Loving Women

SEXUALITIES
General Editor: Gautam Bhan

Other Books in the Series:

Ruth Vanita
Gandhi's Tiger and Sita's Smile
Essays on Gender, Sexuality and Culture

Arvind Narrain and Gautam Bhan (eds)
Because I Have a Voice
Queer Politics in India

Gayatri Reddy
With Respect to Sex
Negotiating Hijra Identity in South India

Rahul Roy
A Little Book on Men

Sunil Gupta
Wish You Were Here
Memories of a Gay Life

A. Revathi
Humaari Kahaniyaan, Humaari Baatein
Hijron ki Jeevaniyon ka ek Sankalan (Hindi)

A. Revathi
Our Lives Our Words
Telling Aravani Lifestories

Arvind Narrain and Alok Gupta (eds)
Law Like Love
Queer Perspectives on Law

Arvind Narrain and Vinay Chandran (eds)
Medicalisation on of Sexual Orientation and Gender Identity
A Human Rights Resource Book (Forthcoming)

Loving Women
Being Lesbian in Unprivileged India

Maya Sharma

YODAPRESS

YODA PRESS
268 A/C Vasant Kunj
New Delhi 110 070
www.yodapress.in

Published in India
by YODA PRESS

First published 2005
Second impression 2014

First Edition ISBN 978-81-903634-1-7

Second Edition ISBN 978-93-82579-8-6-1

Typeset in Aldine401 BT 10.5/12.7
By Excellent Laser Typesetters, Delhi 110 034
Printed at Saurabh Printers Pvt Ltd, New Delhi 110 020
Published by Arpita Das for YODA PRESS

Contents

General Editor's Foreword	vi
Acknowledgements	x
Introduction	1
1. Guddi and Aasu	42
2. Rekha and Dolly	52
3. Vimlesh	61
4. Menaka and Payal	89
5. Manjula and Meeta	102
6. Shiela	123
7. Sabo and Razia	140
8. Mary	157
9. Juhi	168
10. Hasina and Fatima	181

General Editor's Foreword

One has longed for such a book. To be able to speak of class, sexuality, women, communities, movements, and of identities, all at once, in many and varied voices that speak not at, but to, each other, is a rare and wondrous achievement. Few, if any, have broken so many silences simultaneously: speaking of class within the sexuality movement to remind urban, upper class queer communities that other expressions and realities of sexualities exist outside our languages; speaking of sexuality within the women's movement to demand a long-denied recognition and solidarity with the issues of same-sex desiring women; and speaking of lives lived outside definable and bound imaginations of our society that, at times, are so immeasurably suppressed that even the teller can merely allude to the truth rather than simply stating it out loud.

The Sexualities series at Yoda Press could not have found a better addition to our list in Maya's work. In years of being part of the queer and women's movements together, Maya and I have long ached to broaden the understandings of sexuality within both the movements and bring the lives that continued to be silenced even as mainstream India began to speak of some kinds of homosexual lives. This text does that impeccably and in so many critical ways, each of which typifies the aims of this series—it asserts, it introspects, it documents, it testifies, it challenges, and it celebrates.

Living as we do in a sexuality-phobic culture, queer people—along with all those who seek to express any kind of sexuality that is not explicitly bound to marriage and reproduction—have constantly felt the need to prove their existence, and that too only to be able to defend it against charges of abnormality and immorality.

How we testify to our lives, therefore, and how we choose to tell our stories as those located outside heterosexuality (I use the word 'our' as both a tribute to, and in solidarity with, Maya's own insistence to speak about herself as a queer woman) also determines how our stories will be received. Conscious of this need for representation and its importance in queer lives, Maya grapples brilliantly with questions of identity, sexuality, sex, gender, and class, broadening, at each step, the interconnections between all these identities, and reminding us that sexuality cannot be reduced or separated from the complexity of human lives.

The stories of these women challenge any conception of sexuality that limits itself to those that name themselves as gay or lesbian, that are English-speaking, upper-middle class Westernised, or to those that insist that sexuality requires, and indeed is determined solely by, sex. By speaking of relationships between women that go beyond sexual relations alone (though they very much also include them) and that seek to navigate the complicated human geography of two people trying to find ways to love and be with one anther, the stories told in this volume implicitly challenge reductionist and homophobic readings of desire between women. The text asks more fundamental questions: what brings two people together? What kinds of desire are possible between women, and how do these desires find expression? How do we understand the lines between intimacy, friendship, sex, sexuality, and identity? How do power, class, and privilege shape and impact the environments in which these relationships exist? What do each of these mean vis-à-vis seeing the women as political agents, legal citizens, and, simply, human beings?

This challenge comes to the fore in the text's engagement with the identity of 'lesbian'. Recognising both that the word can be 'unrepresentative of the complexities of same-sex relationships, as well as of the ground realities that intersected with caste, class and other factors', Sharma nevertheless uses it in order to firmly continue 'continual efforts to build a politicised identity integral to the rhetoric of gay rights and human rights, since we consider our work to be political and consider lesbians to be valid political subjects, even though we live out the political/legal absurdity of having no status in the eyes of Indian law' (p. 6). Within these lines is an example of the greatest strength of this text. Sharma's engagement remains grounded in the tangible realities of the everyday negotiations that comprise one's lived experience of sexuality, while at the same time recognising the need for community and political identification which may not always be entirely representative, but remains a needed and critical engagement in order to change larger socio-political realities. Such an engagement is incredibly refreshing and path-breaking at a time when, increasingly, identities simply seem to be entrenching themselves in every sphere of our lives from sexuality to caste, class, and religion—the new battlegrounds of modern India.

Sharma makes an effort to reclaim the dynamism of identities, to use them but not be bound by them, to make them sites of individual agency even while using their symbolic and political value as community and political markers. This is a critical point in the evolution of gay and lesbian language and politics in India— until now the movement has seen identities as much-needed shelters and means to find community. It is only now, and slowly, that a questioning of the limitations of identities and their distance from the actual experiences of so many same-sex desiring people in India is actually being acknowledged.

The text also presents a much-needed history of the silence and hostility that same-sex desire has historically received in the women's movement. Placing a hierarchy of grief that declared lesbian rights 'not to be an issue', or, at best, one that must constantly be seen as less important than class, poverty, hunger, and violence, so many women have been silenced within the movement in itself. Sharma's analysis of showing how sexuality has faced much the same resistance that violence issues once did reminds us again of how much movements have to learn from each other and from their own histories. Further, by inextricably linking class and sexuality together, she challenges any contention that sees them as separate concerns that can be pitted against one another and that remain, at all times, mutually exclusive.

Never does Maya exempt herself from any of the questions that she raises in others' lives. Placing her own life-story within the first pages of the introduction itself, Maya reminds us that:

In telling my own life-story, as a feminist I remain committed to transparency. In presenting my subjectivity, I hope to become more conscious, allow room for interrogation and confront my own silences. Including my story here is part of my effort to politicise the personal and also an acknowledgement of the limitations of research as an absolute objective form of knowledge. Self-awareness enabled me to make many subtle, unquantifiable recognitions—I recognised women like me, I recognised my denial and I recognised theirs even as they recognised mine.

In speaking of sexuality, and in telling stories that are so difficult to find, let alone tell, it is Maya's own willingness to constantly question herself, her class, her identity, and her location, that has allowed the women in this volume to speak to her as it did. In the truest sense of the cliché, this text is a journey. It is one that the author and the storytellers have taken together, and it shows in the frankness and simple courage of these tales, and in the magical fact that they exist at all.

This is a book about women. It is about finding desire, of fighting to believe in the right to have and accept such desire, and to find self-descriptions and identities in spaces where no recognition or language exists. It is not simply a story of same-sex desiring women, but at the same time, is proudly and courageously also precisely that. As readers, the greatest tribute one can give to this work is to use the text to embark on our own journeys through sexuality, and take a look at the world around us and realise that everything is not quite as it appears. There are stories at every corner, little subversions against every dominant system, and once in a while, a text that reminds you to constantly keep looking.

GAUTAM BHAN
Delhi, June 2006

Acknowledgements

Grateful thanks to Astraea (National Lesbian Action Foundation), New York, for their financial support, patience, and constant encouragement.

This book would not have been possible without input from a very special person—Shanti. Long time friend, and teacher. Without Shanti the door to the inner *aangan*s of working-class women would never have opened for me.

Shanti has always wanted oral histories to be recorded. Sabo, Razia, Guddi and Aasu, and Sheila were first spoken to by her and only later was I able to go into their lives in depth and record their histories. This effort is as much hers.

I would also like to thank Shernaz Italia, Freny Khodaiji, Indira Pathak, Nighat Gandhi, Padma Singh, Ashley Trellis, Ratna Kapur, Arunesh Mayyar, Satya Nagpaul, Ashwini Sukthankar, Ranjana Padhi, Kanchana Natarajan, Julia Datta and other friends, Rohit and Reenu Sharma, who supported me in many, many ways.

Most of all I am indebted to all the women who agreed to be my contributors, who shared their life experiences with me and opened their homes to me. I am equally indebted to women who shared their stories but did not wish to be written about.

My deepest thanks to my unnamed friend, who edited this work; and without whose constant encouragement this book would not have been completed.

Introduction

In the course of doing research for the project which has ultimately resulted in the present volume, my co-researcher and I were fortunate to come across *Narayan Chitravali* (Shri Nirmal Narayan Mahaprabhu 1999), the Hindi biography of a woman born in 1925 who renounced the world and lived her entire life in an all-woman ashram. The text has an English translation, *Holy Life of Narayan Mahaprabhu* (Dwivedi and Sharma 1996). She is described as being of andro-gynous appearance, performing male tasks and rejecting women's gender roles outright. She had been engaged to be married in Nepal but could not go through with the wedding ceremony and fainted before garlanding the groom—her mother had to complete the ritual. She became so traumatised by the prospect of marrying that she was taken to north India to recuperate. She had a tense relationship with her family after this. It is fascinating that the Hindi text gives an account of Narayan Mahaprabhu's close friendship with a woman, from whom she was inseparable. The two women are described as 'do deh, ek pran' (two bodies, one life-force). This friendship ended before she joined the ashram. No other person outside the family is described in such detail.

Indian culture and society have generally viewed the female body as a site for all kinds of action and reaction, but not as a legitimate site for sexual autonomy or personal agency. Women's sexual experiences are generally understood solely within the established parameters of reproduction. Within this framework, the life experiences of lesbian women have been almost completely invalidated because sex/sexuality are generally understood only in relation to a heterosexual paradigm of oppositional duality, which prescribes gender roles and gendered social codes; those who violate these roles and codes are categorised as transgressive, condemned as obscene, and perceived as appropriate subjects for various forms of persecution and punishment.

In India, women's sexual rights are even now not seen as fundamental or inalienable. Through the women's movement it has become possible to bring into public discourse sexual and domestic violence and make laws for protection against such violations. Victims of and those affected by rape, abduction and sexual slavery, dowry, battery, abuse, foeticide, harassment and gender-biased laws such as those of inheritance and divorce, do come forward to testify, do make their suffering public, do confront their oppressors, be it the family, community or state. With media assistance, they occasionally become role models for others in similar situations. The state has begun to acknowledge, at least theoretically, women's needs—for childcare facilities, workplace safety, equal wages, benefits, right to strike and unionise. There is legislation, albeit controversial, regarding political representation for women, reproductive rights, and sexual health. Women who were earlier seen traditionally as homemakers and their role confined to the domestic sphere, are now being given, by law, facilities that ensure greater participation in the labour market and the public sphere.

But in contrast to this, the movement has adopted a policy of distancing itself from issues related to homosexual women. It must be said though that while it has not extended public/political support, it has indeed extended valuable support privately, taking up individual cases, advocating, intervening, resolving. This support is appreciated by its direct beneficiaries as well as activist groups, yet because it is privately extended it remains unknown to the general public and inaccessible to those who are most urgently in need of it. This mode of support, that simultaneously involves mechanisms of denial, operating under the larger umbrella of cultural silence around issues of alternative sexuality, continues to enmesh homoerotic desire and its practices in phobia and prejudice.

The present volume, which documents the life stories of working-class lesbian women, is rooted in a personal journey of emergence from a space fraught with such silences and half-truths. Its location is the contested sociocultural fissure between the private and the public domain, as well as private and public discourse about alternative sexuality and alternative sexual choices and practices.

Life-Stories and Fragments

We knew that for this project the most effective methodology had also to be the one we most preferred—detailed interviews and one-on-one interactions with the subjects in their own contexts. We were hoping that the life-stories of lesbians from different places in northern India would give us a somewhat fuller understanding of a most marginalised social group; we had hoped for the emergence of a collective voice and at least fragments of visibility through such life-stories. We knew at the outset how difficult it would be to find subjects. But despite the overwhelming void in terms of available research material and statistical data, we decided to commit ourselves to focusing on working-class women in same-sex relationships. We wanted to dispel the myth that lesbians in India were all urban, Westernised and came from the upper and middle classes. And we wanted to create a space for voices with little or no privilege, providing us with an opportunity to share our lived realities with one another and with the others. We hoped our stories would challenge the notion of women as sexual beings without agency. We also hoped to influence the women's movement and work towards an inclusion of lesbian women in the movement.

However, as our work progressed we realised that not all the narratives would qualify as life-stories. Some of them do not go beyond immediate fraught circumstances and the jagged time and space of a brief, intense exchange. When we made an attempt to access the subjects' personal histories or re-establish contact at a later time, we often failed for many different reasons. Sometimes others talked on behalf of the subjects. In at least two cases, our interaction with the subjects was minimal. Yet we continue to use the term 'life-story', and use it interchangeably with the word 'profile'. In these profiles we intuit at least a suggestion of the larger complexity of our subjects' lives, aspirations, pathologies, and struggles, their visions, their coping strategies, their compromises, and modes of resistance.

Initially, I was disturbed by the evident class difference between myself as the researcher and the subjects I hoped to write about. I had spent a great deal of time for several years interacting with working-class women through the women's and the labour movement, and in the course of that time, I have developed close friendships and strong bonds. It was not an easy decision to write about a category of women in whose presence my class gave me automatic entitlements. But my partnership with Shanti, who is from a working-class background, emboldened me. A well-known activist in the women's movement, Shanti's insights and extensive experience were invaluable in the conception, initiation and completion of the project. She unflinchingly made me aware of my class privileges, and yet made me see that those very entitlements, including education, enabled me to go about the task of documenting these stories—I was able to travel, take leave from my regular full-time job, use technology, access infrastructure and make contacts. She was confident that the two of us could together overcome any obstacles we foresaw in undertaking such a project. Her endorsement of my efforts stilled my doubts and self-doubts and allayed my fears.

However, since sexual orientation was not a part of public discourse, unlike other women's issues, my sense of entitlement soon crumbled. This terrain, simultaneously exhilarating and punishing, proved to be a great leveller. I had to begin from the very basics in each case, had to constantly redefine my approach to my subjects and to their contexts, because the material I was seeking often evaded me.

I undertook fieldwork with several different women who were willing to share their skills, energy, resources and time, and supported my ideology and intent. But there were times when circumstances compelled me to work individually. Therefore the reader will encounter both 'I' and 'we' in our text. Writing, transcribing, translating and thinking through issues was always a joint effort.

The general notions we had about the category 'woman', which we had used unquestioningly in an earlier narrative project documenting the life-stories of working-class single women, now itself became problematic when the focus shifted to alternative sexuality. Some of our subjects did not identify as women and used masculine pronouns to define themselves. Most of our subjects had not heard of the word 'lesbian' and asked what language the word came from. They were uncomfortable with and unaccustomed to naming themselves, and resisted affiliating with an unknown identity category that was also a sexual practice. It was a new word. In many ways it reminded us of a time when we had begun to come out to ourselves, and amongst our friends had begun to name, affiliate, identify as lesbians. This utterance changed our perceptions of self and the society, and also functioned as an act of claiming. It became imperative to assert our identity within the women's movement and assert that we too were valid political subjects entitled to rights, freedoms, protections, benefits.

Using the Word 'Lesbian'

It must be pointed out here that at some level we clearly found a single category implied by the use of the word 'lesbian' restrictive, and unrepresentative of the complexities of same-sex relationships, as well as of the ground realities that intersected with caste, class and other factors (which often included marriage, husband and children). But for this project we made a conscious decision to use the word 'lesbian' precisely because it was a word 'so loaded with fear and embarrassment and prejudice, a word shrouded in silence, a whisper that spoke of an identity that must be hidden from others, that frightening word that dare not cross any threshold' (Caleri Report 1999: 17).

When we use the word 'lesbian', we do so consciously as activists involved in the struggle for human rights. We are aware that the hegemonic use of one specific word can effectively silence a diverse and shifting range of sexual/social orientations, identities and practices. During the course of our work, the immensely fraught and complex nature of the material affected us personally and contextually, and at times rendered our preconceptions of identity categories irrelevant. We had to continually adapt, invent, defer and detour while attempting to understand the selfhood of our subjects. However the usage of the word 'lesbian' represents our continual efforts to build a politicised identity integral to the rhetoric of gay rights and human rights, since we consider our work to be political and consider lesbians to be valid political subjects, even though we live out the political/legal absurdity of having no status in the eyes of Indian law.

Influenced, and in fact goaded, by society's denial of same-sex relationships, our use of the word lesbian does mean women who are sexually involved with one another. Yet our collection includes life-stories of women who often do not acknowledge a sexual relationship. While these stories continue to pose an ethical dilemma, we argue that one way to confront the socially-imposed silence regarding issues of alternative sexuality, as well as mechanisms of sexual policing and censorship, was to 'write in' these stories. Through them we attempt to critique a patriarchal system that reifies and perpetuates itself by coercing 'other' sexualities into paradigms of conformity with ideologically driven heterosexuality. However, our own experience while documenting such stories testifies to the falsity of this hegemonic heterosexuality as well as its ongoing subversion. There was rarely an occasion when our query about women who loved women did not bring forth an affirmative response. Almost all of our contacts knew such women in the family, at work places, in the local community, personally, or socially. There were those who identified themselves as one who loved women. But when it came to allowing their life-stories to be printed, they refused. How could they undertake the risk of disclosure and its repercussions without the assurance of external support, when there was no evidence that such support existed, no politicisation of their issues, no collective demand that their needs be addressed? For some, the recognition, validation and fact of lesbian sexuality had been an unuttered impossibility until the actual moment of interview.

These intersecting ambiguities repeatedly confirm that issues regarding alternative sexuality/homosexual women are still being pushed back into the realm of invisibility, silence, denial, erasure, non-existence. Such a posturing within the women's movement ensures the continuation of patriarchal structures in which women's social/sexual identities are deemed valid only in relation to men. It accounts for the absence, within the movement, of reliable public fora committed to addressing the issue of alternative sexual choices.

The levels of social, familial and community denial we encountered during this project, as well as several subjects' insistent categorisation of their homosexual relationships as 'female friendships', can be seen as evasions and deceptions, yet these apparent lies are in fact the existential truth. And no matter how frustrated we sometimes became when the doors were shut in our faces, no matter how agitated we felt at the open denial, we committed ourselves to recording whatever was possible to record the denials, the affirmations and the circumstances and contexts in which they were rooted, for it was the only way to give an authentic picture of the ground realities, of things as they actually are.

My Story

Tiptoeing out of a cool dark room that occasionally sparkled with drops of sunlight that sieved through the moist chiks, the three of us—my older brother, my younger sister and myself—were neither amongst the adults nor the children in the house, like that after-noon sun, neither wet nor dry, indefinable, piercing the shadowy room of sleepers. I did not fit anywhere. Fleeing in the summer afternoons, through the burning courtyard of the house, we passed the neem tree and ran up the incline to the railway tracks behind our house. We competed as to who could walk straight on the tracks for the longest time. When we were caught by the adults, I was chided the most. I was a girl, older than my younger sister. Not a child after all, to indulge in games that did not become a grown girl like me, and to make matters worse I was slapping and kicking! Didn't I know that girls did not raise their hands against boys? Good grown-up girls did not venture into lonely places on lonely afternoons. And when we did go out for the movies or school excursions, I was rarely judged old enough to understand what was good for me. Like my younger sister I had to stay back at home.

No matter what I did, I ended up breaking some rule. Like the railway track that ran ahead of me to the horizon, there was an unquantifiable ideal I always seemed to find outside my reach. I thought marriage would help me attain it. Perhaps it would give me the maturity and the respect that had thus far eluded me. To the family's satisfaction, I 'settled down'. Even better, I soon had a son. Perhaps I was somehow hoping that the ignominy my mother had gone through for bearing five daughters would be countered by the birth of my son. Each girl's birth had been announced by an earthen vessel being struck, so that its dull clap did not spread far and wide. But my only brother's birth was heralded by beating a steel plate so that the good news could resound in all directions.

As I deftly smoothed the creases out of bedspreads and linen and put in place pieces of my household, I began to feel unsettled. No matter what and how much I did to keep the house going, it was never enough, never entirely well done. Also, it was always my responsibility alone. Yet I was given no part in the decision-making. When anger surged up in me, guilt at being angry soon arose in equal measure and haunted me. Nothing I knew or had learnt thus far in my life eased this ongoing conflict.

In the midst of the daily tasks of child-raising and cloistered domesticity, I happened to see women's groups on the television screen, demonstrating on the streets and demanding an end to the violence against women and demanding greater rights for women. The boldness of these groups, bringing private issues into the public arena, initially shocked me and ought to have alienated me. Instead, I was drawn to them. Saheli, one of Delhi's earliest autonomous women's groups, was based in a locality adjoining the one I lived in. I joined them as a volunteer in 1983. It was here that I got the opportunity to work with women survivors of the anti-Sikh riots in 1984. As a result, a long and deep process of internal questioning began. In my search for answers, in 1991 I joined the women's group Jagori as a full-time paid employee.

One of my first assignments involved working in a resettlement colony (slum) in Delhi. The work included local organising as well as documentation of the lives of single women. Women, who were technically considered illiterate, and lived in poverty and at subsistence level, re-educated me in immeasurable ways, on a daily basis. It was one of the most empowering periods of my life. The regular practice of sitting as equals on the ground in a circle as we discussed problems, evolved strategy and planned interventions, urged me to scrutinise my class-based and other privileges.

The first woman I wrote about was Bhavari, a widow in her sixties. She had come to the city from a rural area to find work, like millions of other poor women. Her dark, deeply wrinkled, furrowed visage reflected the intensity of her struggle, and the struggle of others she tried to support, her own children as well as women in need. When others would judge situations and individuals harshly, she would always retain a humane perspective and urge us to do the same. When I sat close to her, she held my chin in her hands and ran her work-worn fingers along my face and arms. 'My husband did not ever ask me how I am, what I drink, eat and wear, he never loved me like this...' (Bhaiya 1996: 45). She seemed to be expressing my own yearning, what she described was that familiar. But at the same time I became aware of something new, an unexpected sensation of pleasure at her touch. I recognised with a shock that I was experiencing arousal through the caress of a woman. The feeling brought back the memory of a dark staircase in a convent school. A memory which I thought had died with a phase I had 'outgrown'. That day when I came back home from the resettlement colony, conflicted and dazed, there was a great churning within. But externally, nothing had changed.

Later, in my meetings with more women, traces of what I had absorbed would return to me, like the weathered touch of Bhavari. Listening to the women, I began to see how the power of social structures impacts our most intimate relationships. A larger pattern in our individual and varied lives, reflected in the identical words we used in the telling of our stories—'caged', 'good woman', 'bad woman', began to appear before me. The daily presence of women who put at stake their precarious resources in order to change their lives inspired me to change mine. I gathered the courage to speak to my son and step out of my marriage of 16 years.

But the turning point came almost invisibly. It came when I listened to Bhavari talk of a relationship between two women. Simply and without judgement, she said that these two women met one another in the fields away from their homes and families. 'They loved one another dearly. They could not live without seeing one another...' (ibid. 1996: 46). I was fascinated, but it was very difficult for me to document this story. I had just begun to find myself. I was afraid. It was only towards the end of the project that I was able to incorporate the account.

Even though I acknowledged my love for women, I was living in fear. I had only Bhavari to go to. Other than her, there was no one I knew even in the women's movement with whom I could openly talk. It was only later, in private conversation and through carefully coded disclosures, that I learnt that there were many women like me in the movement. I also began to see how, when dealing with issues in the movement, factors like class, caste, marital status were acknowledged as crucial variables but there was rarely any mention of sexual preference.

Finally, my involvement with another woman strengthened me. I was no longer alone. As we negotiated our relationship, we received support from women like us was who were similarly half-hidden. What we often missed was an outer, larger affirming space in which we could be ourselves without pretensions, disguises or evasions.

In telling my own life story, as a feminist I remain committed to transparency. In presenting my subjectivity, I hope to become more conscious, allow room for interrogation and confront my own silences. Including my story here is part of my effort to politicise the personal and also an acknowledgement of the limitations of research as an absolute objective form of knowledge. Self-awareness enabled me to make many subtle, unquantifiable recognitions—I recognised women like me, I recognised my denial and I recognised theirs even as they recognised mine.

Our own life-stories were a valuable resource in this project. We were able to break the barrier of silence and the taboos that surround the lives of our subjects by sharing our own lives with them. The women who shared their lives with us took a risk, knowing that such disclosure might have disastrous and punitive consequences for them, socially and personally. I add my own story to theirs to honour their courage.

The Politics of Utterance

Caleri (Campaign for Lesbian Rights), a Delhi-based non-funded autonomous group of lesbians, gay men, bisexuals and heterosexuals, was formed in December 1998 following broad-based protests against the Shiv Sena's attacks on cinema halls screening Deepa Mehta's film *Fire*. This right-wing political party demanded that the film be withdrawn because it contained explicit scenes of a physical relationship between two married sisters-in-law living in a joint family under the same roof. Such depictions, according to the Shiv Sena and its supporters, were a manifestation of promiscuous Western morality that would corrupt Indian values and Indian women. Caleri took active part in the public rally organised to protest against the Sena vandalism. This rally was organised to protect the democratic constitutional right to freedom of artistic expression. The unqualified homophobia of the Sena cadre and the political establishment is evidenced in statements compiled in the Caleri Report (1999).

'Why are such films made here? They can be made in the US or other Western countries. A theme like lesbianism does not fit in the Indian atmosphere.'
—Union Minister for Home, L.K. Advani.

'Ek aurat is doing intercourse with the other. On camera. What message are we sending the public?'
—Shiv Sena Delhi Unit chief Jai Bhagwan Goel.

'There can be no argument that lesbianism is unnatural and is regarded as such the world over.'
—Former Union Minister for Information and
Broadcasting, Sushma Swaraj.

'What do you get by showing lesbianism? As it is, the institution of marriage is breaking down. This will make it worse.'
—Jai Bhagwan Goel

'Has lesbianism spread like an epidemic that it should be portrayed as a guideline to unhappy wives not to depend on their husbands?'
—Shiv Sena chief Bal Thackeray

'Thanks to the film, even those who didn't know anything about lesbianism are now being introduced to it.'
—Shiv Sena MLA Shrikant Sarmalkar

'Do we have lesbian culture in our families? Surely, this film has put all of us in a shameful light. *Humko chullu bhar paani mein doob marna chahiye.*'

—Shiv Sena leader Madhukar Sarpotdar

The uproar created by the responses to *Fire* and the visible presence of lesbians among those who protested the Sena's acts of vandalism is vividly described by Sandhya Luther, a lesbian activist, in '*Fire! Fire!* It's the Lesbians!' in the Caleri Report:

> By the morning of December 8 it had all happened. The word 'lesbian' was on the front page of every newspaper I picked up in Delhi. LESBIAN. It looked odd and out of place. Why was a word like that being tossed around? A word so loaded with fear and embarrassment and prejudice, a word shrouded in silence, a whisper that spoke of an identity that must be hidden from others, that frightening word that dare not cross any threshold, was on that winter morning landing at the doorsteps of millions of households in many parts of the country. At my colleagues' doors. At my parents'. At their neighbours'. At my landlord's. My neighbour was going to read it. The Mother Dairy man was going to read it. The woman in the workshop, My sister-in-law.... They were all going to pick up their morning newspaper and stare at a word they had possibly not seen earlier in print, and never given much thought to, and wonder what it was doing on Page One. And Three. And in editorials. And letters to editors. And in Special Features. Not just that day but days and weeks and weeks after December 8.

> As we piled printed page on page into our clippings file, we were left feeling a little bewildered. It took just one poster, one banner and a few scared but brave women in a public protest of eighty other slogans, posters and hundreds of people, to generate all this public discussion and media glare. One brave act of holding up a placard that said 'Indian and Lesbian' had caused such a *hulchul*, such journalistic diarrhoea. Why did the mere announcement of one's existence cause such a cacophony?

> We are supposed to have been dwelling in comfortable silence for so many centuries, Silence about our existence, a conspiracy

of silence. A social pact. Don't let us know! Don't let your family know who you are and how you live, not many of your friends, certainly not your co-workers, not your boss, as also neighbours, not to mention (neither last nor least) your landlord...never, never, never speak about who you are or how you live. Silence. That will protect you. It does not matter that none of the rites of passage of your life will ever be acknowledged, let alone celebrated. That you must hide your love and happiness as well as your heartbreak and loneliness in wells of silence. How can this silence, which is not self-chosen, even be empowering? Why is it glorified and perpetuated? This silence is not spiritual—it will not bring you inner peace. It is not powerful, it is the poorest of defences.... It is to live a life filled with lies.... It is forever a weapon in the hands of others....

On December 7 we were breaking the social contract. Some of us were taking great personal risk in holding up those posters in the middle of a sea of candles, in the face of flashing cameras. Interestingly, some of the individuals and groups who had joined in to protest the attack on "freedom of speech and expression' and 'democratic rights' were upset and vitriolic about the same freedoms being extended to a minority in a peaceful and demo-cratic public protest. We were severely criticised before and after: why did we have to be visible, how did we dare to use the word 'lesbian', why were we insisting *Fire* had anything to do with lesbianism when the filmmaker herself was denying it, why were we breaking The Silence? Why were we talking about People Like Us, who should never be seen, even by candlelight?

Similarly, lesbian activist Ashwini Sukthankar comments in the Introduction to her *Facing the Mirror: Lesbian Writing from India* (1999):

In early December, just weeks before the publication date of this book, the Shiv Sena launched a frenzied assault on screenings of Deepa Mehta's film *Fire*. Some lesbians in cities across India chose to be visible, as lesbians, in protests against the Sena violence—though individuals connected to the film claimed it was not a lesbian-themed work, we wanted to emphasise that the attacks on it were impelled by homophobia.

We were accused by segments of the media of having 'hijacked' these protests by the mere act of being visible, or of having 'derailed' the 'larger' debate of artistic freedom and democratic rights simply by being present. And a simple placard that declared its bearer to be 'Indian and Lesbian' earned an entire community much censure for alleged militancy and cultural anarchy.

Those of us who live out the twin truths of being Indian and lesbian know what we are and where we come from.... The reaction to our living presence has been painful to witness, a further reminder that the 'culture of tolerance' in which we live is fictitious. But it reinforces our belief in this book.... We will not be shamed into pretending that we do not exist.

After the *Fire* uproar, Caleri decided to make lesbian issues visible in the public domain of human rights in India and consciously strategise towards this goal, within the larger frame of the women's movement. Since violence against women was one of the globally chosen themes for International Women's Day 2000, while planning meetings for the public march we brought up the need to include the demand for lesbian rights.

We cited feature stories and reports published in a Malayam fortnightly named *Sameeksha* in its issues of 28 June–11 July 1998, and 1–15 June 1999, entitled 'Same Sex (Female) Lovers Commit Suicide' and 'Lesbian Suicides Continue...'; the writer was K.C. Sebastian. But the Left mass-based women's groups resisted the inclusion of the word 'lesbian' in the literature to be distributed on 8 March. The logic was that the name of the group Campaign for Lesbian Rights could not go on the pamphlets because they would be distributed in working-class localities where people were still not ready to openly discuss homosexuality. Always in search of sensationalism, the press would pay attention only to the sexuality issues; ultimately, the flaunting of sexual terminology would detract from important political issues that needed to be the focus of media attention. Also, the issue of sexuality had been raised rather late in the joint forum. To suddenly change the agenda now would not be possible. Countering this argument were others like us who said that there were issues like education that had not come up right in the beginning but were nevertheless included later, indicating that time was not a significant factor for the exclusion of issues of sexuality. We argued that the women's movement is known for taking up issues as and when the need arose to address them. There was no debate or deadline, for example, when it came to campaigning for the rights of dalit (oppressed caste) women. Why were we then setting time limits for bringing up the issue of violence against lesbians?

Subsequent to these meetings, various women's groups met again to resolve the conflict. Here it was decided that instead of alienating and factionalising the participating groups who could not come to a consensus regarding the need to publicly press for lesbian rights, discussions and meetings amongst the different groups could be held later to discuss homosexuality and evolve an understanding on the issue. At one such meeting it was shared that the lack of information about lesbians and the absence of documentation of a sufficient and specific number of cases of lesbian life prevented women's groups from going against the majority voice in Indian culture. In response, we made presentations. We mostly described individual cases that had already been reported in the press. The stories we knew of lacked a face; women's own voices and the context within which they lived their daily lives were missing. We ourselves had no idea what happened to most of the women following the exposure and the outcry raised by public scandal. We also became aware that working-class voices were almost completely missing from among the groups involved in gay rights activism. The fact that the women who came into the public gaze as a result of the sexuality issue were mostly women from the working class becomes even more ironical in view of such a situation.

The silencing/distancing/censorship of homosexual issues within public discourse has resulted in the formation and emergence of a few gay rights groups within cities that work publicly on issues of sexuality, sexual rights and sexual health. The growing movement for the prevention of HIV/AIDS has also brought attention to sexuality/homosexuality. Globalisation and liberalisation have contributed in no small part to a general opening up of new socio-economic and cultural spaces, within which the media has become more liberal and widened its focus to include sexual issues that were previously considered taboo. Our impulse to undertake a project on alternative sexuality was catalysed by this wider focus, which was now making possible articulations that earlier had been impossible. The energy of dissent as well as the ongoing dialogue with women's groups regarding the issue of lesbian rights motivated us to take up work that would do precisely this: render lesbians visible.

We began to see that the issue of lesbian existence/non-existence, so contentious in forums where women's groups have brought up women's rights and sexual rights, had a pattern. The core arguments around visibility and utterance have been simmering for at least a decade. The Caleri Report (1999: 4) sums up the activist position:

> The focus on lesbian rights was for a reason—to articulate and nurture the troubled connections in/with the women's move-ment, to talk about the social suppression of women's sexuality in general…the formation of Caleri was seen as a step towards dispelling the myths around lesbianism and establishing it as part of an existing reality in our society and culture.

As stated earlier, perceived and treated as a threat to existing systems and structures, any public assertion of homosexual rights within the mass-based women's movement is generally silenced with the ra-tionale that sexual preference is a private issue; thus recreating the patriarchal separation of the public and private spheres.

The kind of silence and distancing that takes place can be seen by comparing the movement's response to two instances of sexual and emotional violence against women. One case involved the fate of Mamta and Monalisa—two young women from Orissa. Their case was detailed in a 1998 fact-finding report by the AIDS Bhedbhav Virodhi Andolan (ABVA) (1999: 15). Both women knew that their same-sex relationship was not acceptable to their families, and had filed an affidavit for a partnership deed so that they could live together. The imminent job transfer of Monalisa's father, a govern-ment employee, led the women to attempt suicide because they knew that they would be separated. They consumed insecticide and also slashed their wrists. Discovered while still alive, they were taken to the hospital. Monalisa died on the way, while Mamta survived and was later forced to undergo psychiatric treatment. While Mamta's father stated in a letter to ABVA, 'For your information, this is not a case of homosexuality', Monalisa's grandfather stated, 'It is a case of lesbianism'. In their joint suicide note the women had expressed the wish to be cremated together on the same pyre.

The other case was also from Orissa. Anjana Mishra, the 30-year-old victim, was the estranged wife of an Indian Forest Service officer and the mother of his two sons.Mishra strongly resisted her husband's attempt to separate her from her two children and have her secured within a mental asylum. In 'My Story' (*Week*, 7 February 1999), Mishra writes, 'Utkal Mahila Samiti, the leading women's organisation in the state, actively took up the case and pressured the Human Rights Protection Cell (HRPC) to rescue me from Ranchi; I had spent nine months and ten days in the gloom and horror of the lunatic asylum.' Later she bravely fought off the state Advocate-General Indrajeet Ray's attempts to rape her. When it became clear that she could not be compelled to retract her charges of molestation and attempt to rape against Ray, she was brutally gangraped by three men at Barang on 9 January 1999, while en route to Cuttack with a journalist friend to meet her lawyer.

The assault took place at the same time as the Mamta-Monalisa suicide attempt. Women's groups supported Mishra' struggle for justice within the state, and organised a public demonstration at Orissa Bhavan in New Delhi, protesting the gang rape, but were totally silent about the Mamta-Monalisa case. Indeed, a cautious acknowledgement of violence against lesbians has mostly come in the form of letters, personal comments and private communication, after meetings and conferences. For instance, in February 1992 a letter to the editor was signed by over three dozen women in response to a report that appeared on 29 January 1992 in the national daily *Indian Express*, headlined 'Lesbian Group in Kerala School'. The letter stated that the suspension of these girls from school on the grounds of homosexuality was a violation of their fundamental rights. Some of these signatories were from the women's groups but they chose to sign as individuals.

A decade later, at a Women's Studies conference in Bhubaneshwar in 2002, one continued to hear remarks such as, 'Yes, there are lesbians within my own family, nothing wrong with them, really.'

At a Human Rights Conference in Panchgani from 26 December 2001 to 1 January 2002, there was a private discussion on how difficult it was for lesbian women to cope with the guilt they felt because their religion or culture declared their sexual practices to be wrong/sinful, and what kind of support and advice should be offered in such situations.

In September 1993, lesbianism had been the focus of a programme in the woman-oriented series 'Shakti', telecast by the Zee channel. Several women wrote to the producers in the weeks following, using pseudonyms or sending the letters unsigned. 'I am caught in a peculiar conflict. You tell me what a girl should do if she falls in love with another girl. Please reply, I am putting a false name...'; 'I am a 20-year-old married girl...my husband loves me a lot, my in-laws are good too, my problem is that I have fallen in love with a girl. She is married also...because of this many times I end up fighting with my husband...when we make love I think of her, what am I to do, please tell me something....'

Alienated from their own experiences in a deeply heterosexist society, these are the voices of women who desperately seek affirmation. Ten years later, if activist voices in the women's movement still continue to ask, 'Do negative experiences with men make women opt for lesbian sexuality?' or 'Why does homosexuality have to be talked about so much and so openly when it is a private issue?' (Caleri Report 1999: 27), one can certainly say that it is high time for the movement to talk more often more openly, and take a collective, public stand on the issue.

In 1994, the mass-based, leftist National Federation of Indian Women (NFIW) formally demanded that the Prime Minister ban a conference on homosexuality being held in Mumbai, alleging that such activity was a sign of 'decadent Western culture'. The Delhi-based group Jagori wrote to other women's groups, seeking their response on this 'controversial' issue: 'We are aware of the difficulties surrounding this issue but this should not stop us from informing ourselves of the conditions and struggles of people who have been silenced by the arrogance of certain views....' The letter concludes, 'We hope that you will respond soon. We will take the responsibility of circulating your responses to all of you who would like to be informed on the issue.'[1]

In response to a letter from Caleri in 2001, NFIW wrote:

When the question of making these groups [lesbian groups] a part of the existing joint platform was raised on the eve of International Women's Day in the year 2000, we had pointed out that it might not be possible for us—at least for the time being—to include the issue of lesbian rights among those issues which were to be highlighted on International Women's Day. Surely you would concede to us the right to focus on those issues, which in our assessment, should be urgently taken up by the women's movement. The collective opinion of our organisation was and still is: that the issue of lesbian rights is not such an issue.

The letter adds, 'We are opposed to any intervention by the state in the matter of adult lesbian relationships.'[2]

In fact, when the state itself is an offender, the nature of such intervention is founded on a fundamental paradox that lesbians in India live out daily: their complete absence as legal subjects. Since they do not exist in the eyes of the law, they do not violate the law. But nor do they have any political or social rights. Section 377 of the Indian Penal Code, that criminalises homosexuality is as follows:

Whoever voluntarily has carnal intercourse against the order of nature with any man, woman or animal shall be punished with imprisonment for life, or with punishment of either description for a term which may extend to 10 years and shall also be liable to fine. Explanation: Penetration is sufficient to constitute the carnal intercourse necessary to the offence described in this section.

This muddy rhetoric criminalises what is perceived to be male homosexual activity, that is, the act of sodomy and its sexual prac-titioners who are going 'against the order of nature'. Lesbianism is not specified as a criminal act, but since it is perceived as 'unnatural', it is illegal by analogy and association. As lesbian activist Ashwini Sukthankar remarks:

Section 377 of the Indian Penal Code makes homosexual acts between men illegal but does not technically have lesbianism within its purview since the legal definition of intercourse requires penetration...the invisibility conferred on us by the law—our special share of the country's colonial legacy—does not necessarily result in lesbians being 'legal' and therefore having legal recourse to fighting discrimination and harassment. On the contrary, invisibility means that the fact of our existence is still more shocking when it is revealed, and the very law that seems to ignore the reality of lesbian existence is employed to crush it out (Sukthankar 1999: xiii, xiv).

Crushing out also takes place in other ways. In the same context of publicly demonstrating in favour of lesbian rights on 8 March, the national, mass-based leftist women's group Akhil Bharatiya Janwadi Mahila Samiti wrote to Caleri: 'A banner saying Campaign for Lesbian Rights will not only cause confusion about the issues we have agreed to highlight but will divert attention from them. You have described this as "sacrificing lesbians". It can equally be interpreted as sacrificing the issues of poor women.'[3]

Thus, according to such logic, sexual difference is responsible for confusion. It also implies that the lesbian woman and the poor woman are two different categories of women. And if by chance a lesbian woman is poor, it is her poverty that will be foregrounded and addressed, not her sexual orientation. Similar intersecting personal, social and economic needs, are summed up in their full complexity by Preeti, one of the first women we interviewed:

> I have only one dream—a house of my own and my lover living in it with me. One bedroom will do, and there is not even any need for a dining room. But there should be a drawing room with a television and a good music system and there should be a balcony where I can sit and read the newspaper. Even if I become a millionaire, the size of my house will not change. Otherwise there will be no peace, life will be an endless stream of desires....
>
> But that is a dream. Consider our reality, our fate as two women who want to live together. Suppose I sign all my assets over to

my lover and she signs all her assets over to me, and later we split up for this or that reason. Who will be accountable? How will the claims be settled? If a man and woman marry and get into conflict, there are laws, families, the whole of society to intervene, there are systems and procedures. One can go to the courts and get some compensation. But a same-sex relationship is illegal, and moreover it is a punishable offence, I have heard. There is no security, no provision for people like us....

I have had so many friendships and relationships but not a single one has lasted. After making all kinds of promises, my partners have gone back on their commitment to me. They get married, saying that marriage, husband, children, establishing their own households, is the right way to live. Once they make the choice of marriage, they start to say that people like us are wrong, that it is not possible for two women to live together. How does one deal with this? And I am there as a special invitee to these weddings, watching, hurting inside while other guests think I am sad because I am not the one getting married! Tell me, what is one to do?

I am working extra jobs to save money so that I can have a sex change operation. Only this will enable my lover and me to be part of the mainstream as a couple. We will be acceptable to society. In India even love marriages are by and large unacceptable, what chance is there for people like us? Our relationships will never be acceptable. Having a sex change operation is not about having more enjoyable sex, that is not the point at all though most people think it is. My lover wants me to have the operation, she has chosen a man's name for me already.

Such a Long Journey

In the mid-1980s, when violence against women was slowly being recognised as an issue that needed to be addressed, the Left-party-affiliated women's organisations considered wife-beating to be another form of violence which demonstrated the corrosive and degenerative aspects of capitalist society rather than as a result of the unequal power relationships within the domestic realm. Activists Nandita Shah and Nandita Gandhi write, 'In this context at that time a member of the Janwadi Mahila Samiti (New Delhi) had said, "It would be politically incorrect to pit women against men. We would definitely take up the issue of wife-beating and help individual women but not call a morcha (demonstration) until the time both men and women see the need for a strong joint action"' (Gandhi and Shah 1991: 66). They add that the women's group Pennuramai Iyyakkam (Chennai) felt that taking up wife-beating as a campaign issue requires women to be active and vigilant everyday. At the grassroots level the issue would require tremendous energy time and preparation. For the time being they would help individual women. Another example cited is of SEWA (Self Employed Women's Association) Ahmedabad, which considers itself primarily a workers' organisation, and addresses wife-beating on an individual level, with the reasoning that questions relating to domestic violence would splinter already conflicted families and detract from the questions relating to worker's rights and labour. Similarly, the Chattisgarh Mahila Mukti Morcha took up the issue of wife-beating by establishing a sub-committee to deal with cases on an individual level (ibid.: 67).

Almost 20 years later, one can hear a similar ring in arguments for the rights of the lesbian women. The problem remains unresolved: the larger collective women's movement with a public face is unwilling to be seen as openly supportive of lesbian rights and of the few individuals/groups within the movement who campaign for gay rights in general. The movement's resistance to addressing violence against lesbians and publicly discussing lesbian issues, as well as putting lesbian issues on the political agenda, still holds that such politicisation should be postponed for a later time, presumably when there is a greater level of societal awareness and acceptance of homosexuality. Often the argument is that the movement should not be 'pitting women against men', or 'causing confusion', 'sidetracking', 'hijacking', or 'diverting attention'.

In contrast to the mass-based women's groups, the autonomous women's groups have had a somewhat different response to the issue of lesbian rights. Between 1989–91, a new articulation had been shaped: 'single woman' was beginning to be recognised as a valid, self-chosen identity. Lesbians were seen as belonging to this category. At the Autonomous Women's Movement Conference held in Calicut in 1990 an informal session on single women was held, and perhaps for the first time the word 'lesbian' was used. A middle-class woman identified herself as a lesbian in that meeting. After the Calicut conference, the woman's group Jagori began research on single women, but did not openly address lesbian issues within these parameters. It mentions lesbians as one of the categories of single women but it did not openly address lesbian issues within these parameters. Nor did the category 'single women' accommodate more complex positions, such as those of married lesbians with or without children.

The Northern Regional Conference of the Women's Movement held in Kanpur in 1993 had a session on sexuality, but women standing outside the room predicted dismissively that such a session would contain 'nothing more than lesbianism'. Anticipating such comments, we who were organising the workshop on behalf of Jagori had committed to a strategy: to avoid a predominant focus on lesbian issues, and in order not to detract/distract from more general issues, we ordained that women who were not 'out' but did self-identify as lesbians would keep a low profile during the discussions. Also, in the interest of ensuring that this strategy was not interrogated, we excluded an out lesbian who we felt would not comply with our plan. Ironically, during the session someone asked about women who did not marry, 'What about their sexual desire?' We had created a space where such issues could be interrogated, yet lesbian issues could not. Today in retrospect we are aghast that we thought of raising the issue of lesbian sexuality in the session on single women, and we acknowledge the extent of internal and external homophobia that compelled us to strategise in this questionable manner.

But the Fifth Women's Movement Conference in Tirupati in 1994 was different. For the first time 'sexuality' was a separate workshop theme, with lesbianism as a sub-theme. There was an open discussion led by a mother who fully supported her daughter's relationship with a woman. But the session turned stormy when a resolution supporting lesbian rights was formulated. Inconclusive and acrimonious debate prevented this resolution from being passed.

When a statement about accepting lesbian sexuality was framed, a group of women protested by writing a letter which said that lesbianism was unnatural and abnormal. For many participants, the resolution's somewhat ambiguous phrasing—'We attempted to understand the importance of sexual preference of women and resolved that the women's movement should create the space for lesbian women to share their frustrations and aspirations'—did not authentically reflect the workshop processes, in which a majority of attendees openly expressed support for lesbian women. A note of dissent was made with the following statement, 'Women are not given a real choice to explore and choose their own sexuality. We believe that every woman should have the individual freedom to explore and choose her sexuality' (*A Report* 1994: 58). At this conference, a special meeting of self-identified lesbians and bisexual women was held for the first time. A meeting was planned for the next day. But a poster with the information about the time and venue of the meeting was torn off the walls. For several reasons, the second meeting could not take place, but the first meeting had opened up possibilities in terms of organising and networking (ibid.: 59).

The NGO Forum at the Fourth World Conference on Women at Beijing in 1995 created history. A 'lesbian tent' was pitched right in the middle of the conference venue. The discussions were constant and energetic, and we spent some time with a distraught mother who had questions about homosexuality that she wanted answered, so that she could better understand her gay son. However, here too not all supporters of sexual rights supported the demand for lesbian rights. It was hinted that lesbians claiming public space and politicising the issue of their rights could interfere with the critically important wider agendas of the conference (Rothschild and Long 2000: 65).

The 1997 National Conference of the Women's Movement held in Ranchi, states in its declaration: 'We support the empowerment of women who may be further marginalized by other facets of their identities: adivasis (tribals), dalits, (oppressed caste) poor and working class women, disabled women, religious minorities, lesbians, bisexuals' (*A Report* 1997: 6). And yet the Bihar State Coordinating Committee organizing the conference deleted the word 'lesbian' from its invitation letter, because the members felt strongly that the inclusion of this word and a specific session on lesbian sexuality would have alienated many women's groups and individual women who then would not attend the conference. They also felt that women would not want to work as volunteers at a conference which included a focus on homosexuality.

The stand that lesbian issues and lesbians themselves not be made publicly visible within the women's movement, has been based on the following arguments: it is for the greater good of the movement; the presence of lesbians (since they are unacceptable publicly) will fragment whatever collectivity has been established over the years, fewer women will associate with the movement, fewer groups will participate, and mainstream and state support will be seriously compromised. The women's movement has adopted a paternalistic tone, insisting that it knows best, that it will raise the issue of lesbian rights at an opportune moment and with the right strategy, (how the opportune moment/change will be brought about is never clearly stated). The movement is still resorting to the constant alibi that other issues are more worthy of support than the 'private' domain of lesbian rights. The movement's support of individual cases in- volving lesbian rights is no doubt invaluable, but it does not initiate urgently needed collective change, and in fact helps to maintain status quo. This manner of tacit support does not advocate social and legal interventions when lesbian rights are violated, for it ensures that lesbians continue to be perceived as socially unacceptable single women without legal status, political agency, rights, needs, claims, benefits and protections. Ironically, the women's movement seems to be afraid of being isolated from the mainstream activist move- ment if it is seen to visibly, publicly, demand rights for those who are an isolated and invisible minority within the movement in particular as well as within society in general.

Thus accustomed to living as absences, we were not surprised at the absence of statistical data. In fact, until 2001 there were no statistics on lesbians in India. That year, I learnt from my friends Bina Fernandez and Gomathy N.B. that a study on violence against lesbians was being conducted by the Research Centre on Violence Against Women in the Tata Institute of Social Sciences in Mumbai, lesbians were included as research subjects for the first time, a rare acknowledgement of legitimate identity, and an even rarer articulation of lesbians as valid juridico-legal subjects entitled to justice and protection under Indian law.

A Giant Step

'Women's rights are human rights'—this feminist/activist slogan may appear to be a tautological statement, but its reiteration is necessary, for human rights discourse did not always protect women's rights adequately. The collective trauma of two world wars was the context within which the international laws on human rights were framed. The understanding that no one 'shall be subjected to arbitrary interference with his privacy, family...'[4] allowed the oppression of women within the family to go unaddressed. The focus remained on human rights violations in the public sphere by the state, including arrests, torture and curtailment of freedom of expression.

The adoption of the Convention on Elimination of all Forms of Discrimination against Women (CEDAW) in December 1979 created the possibility of change. At the UN World Conference on Human Rights held in 1993, consolidated pressure from women activists to recognise violence against women as a breach of human rights led to the Draft Declaration on the Elimination of Violence against Women, later adopted by the UN General Assembly. Article 1 of the Declaration defines 'violence against women' as 'any gender-based violence that results in physical, sexual or psychological harm or suffering to women, including threats of such acts, coercion or arbitrary deprivation of liberty whether occurring in public or private'.

In 1995, the Beijing Platform of action further acknowledged in Para 18 that violence against women 'is a manifestation of the historically unequal power relations between men and women'. However, paragraphs 95 and 96 of the same document limit women's rights over their bodies to control over reproduction, without any focus on sexual agency, and confine the definition of family and partnership to the heterosexual model, under the umbrella of state-recommended population control policies. Women are denied the right to self-determination and merely exist as physical sites of production and male will.

Lesbian rights, which by their very nature foreground women as autonomous sexual beings imbued with selfhood, reason and desire, thus do not confine the issue to a particular sexuality or identity category but open up possibilities for an overall redefinition of women, women's rights and human rights. We hope this study of working-class lesbian lives contributes in some way towards the larger processes of rendering human rights fundamental and in-alienable for all women.

Finding a Way

The general sociocultural perception that sexuality is a private matter influenced our strategies and dominated our strategies in each case we undertook to document. Word of mouth, personal networking, newspaper reports, and to a large extent intuition, the one variable that cannot be quantified, were some of the means by which we identified potential subjects. Our position as activists in both the labour movement and the women's movement affiliated us to marginalised groups, and our understanding of various kinds of marginality helped to sensitise us to the extreme marginality of our working-class lesbian subjects.

Our project, begun in June 2001, was completed over two years. Documentation and fieldwork were done simultaneously, depend-ing on what material we collected, in what form and how much. We compiled fifteen stories but the final selection has been re-stricted to ten. We have applied various methodologies, and have tried to present stories which reflect different religions, regions, castes, ages and literacy levels. The common factor is that all our subjects are working-class women.

In eight stories, the subjects openly acknowledged their same-sex attraction, though they use varied terms to describe their homo-sexual relationships. Two stories focus on women who denied being in a same-sex relationship and categorised their relationship as friendship. We have tried to interpret our subjects' gestures, expres-sions, emotions and implied statements, apart from recording their own words. The subjects' circumstances and contexts have been described in necessary detail. Two stories emerged from fact-finding visits to the subjects' homes after the relationship had been exposed in the newspapers and had become a cause for public scandal.

Many women simply trusted us from the start and shared their stories verbally, but did not want to be written about and absolutely refused to give us permission to publish anything they had said. Of the 20 participants at a workshop that we conducted to identify lesbian women, 16 admitted to having relationships with women. Some of them continued in these relationships in spite of their own marriages or the marriages of their lovers. Inadvertently, the workshop opened up a space for two women to address their anger. 'In this very room,' one of them said with sadness, 'we had vowed to be together but you got married. . . .' In contrast, another woman described how she had intercepted the prospective husband coming to see her, and told him she would not marry him. Rather than directly say no to her family and thus risk losing their support, she took direct action in her own behalf. The man withdrew his proposal.

With some subjects we experienced an instant recognition and camaraderie, a sense of being on the same journey while traversing different paths. But we also faced instances when the subjects themselves denied or were silent about being in a same-sex relationship, yet this was explicitly disclosed by their friend or acquaintance. Often we did not get the opportunity to reveal the real nature of our inquiry to our sources, and we could not articulate exactly what we were looking for. We usually phrased it as 'single women' or 'a woman who lives with another woman'.

The silence around homosexuality is slowly, distortedly, in fragments, being broken in the media, and while we question the skewed and partial media representation, its dependence on stereotype and its hesitant imaging, we simultaneously acknowledge its use and appreciate its existence, for it brings same-sex love into the public domain and the realm of public discourse. Critically, in more than one instance it enabled us to locate subjects, and made fact-finding interventions possible. However, the media remains in general more committed to the sensational and catastrophic, and rarely does follow-up stories or in-depth investigations that might create more awareness in the readership/viewership, with regard to homosexuality. After the disclosure and public scrutiny of lesbian scandal, the women simply cease to exist in mainstream consciousness.

On 8 September 2001, the national Hindi daily *Navbharat Times* carried a front-page story about two women who ran away together from their homes in Indore on 1 September. They went to a town in a different state and got married to one another, They then took shelter within a popular religious sect. From here they were forcibly retrieved by the police after their families lodged a Missing Person's Report. They were returned to their respective homes in Indore on 7 September. After the terrorist attacks on New York's World Trade Towers on 11 September, the national media was fully occupied and lesbian elopement did not make the front pages. Later, on our fact-finding visit, I learnt from the Indore-based reporter who filed the story that he had been asked by the newspaper to also send photos of the two women. But fortunately these were not published. Another magazine then published their pictures in an article. The other half of this story, in which families, communities and the state conspire to silence the sexual lives of lesbian subjects even further, in defence of family/community honour that has been transgressed by the subjects, found no space at all in the paper.

Neither does the media ever report that women in same-sex relationships do protest against the violation of their freedom. For instance one subject, Dolly, had filed a complaint against her lover Rekha's family for harassing her and preventing her from meeting Rekha. When a police constable arrived to look into the complaint, Rekha's uncle allegedly bribed him to turn around and walk away. We wrote to the SDO as a women's group, informing him of the real situation and requesting him to intervene and ensure that the two women be allowed to freely move about, meet one another and associate with anyone they wished to. There was no response from him. Dolly was featured along with cases of 'lesbian marriage' in a popular weekly Hindi newsmagazine (*India Today* 19–26 December 2001: 43). I recognised our subject in the photograph as it was the same one that the local reporter had shown me on my visit there. In the magazine article, Dolly acknowledges that she had several relationships with women prior to the one with Rekha. The article also carried a picture of two domestic workers who had married one another. Though the text claimed that the women had their parents' support, it does not describe how the partnerships have been viewed by the extended family or the community. Half-a-dozen such marriages were reported in the Chattisgarh region in 2000.

Thus, the erasure of selfhood and denial of sexual autonomy is accomplished not just literally by mechanisms of policing, censoring and connivance by the family, community and state, but also through these agents conspiring to inflict upon lesbian subjects the emotional violence of sustained equivocation—simultaneously inscribing and erasing, acknowledging the transgression but at the same time denying that it took place for homosexual reasons.

In our attempt to speak, and to document our subjects' voices, we became aware that various silencing mechanisms would always continue to intervene. We struggled not only with limited funds and facilities, but also with contextual pressures that we anticipated yet were unprepared for. We had to accept that frank, extended and honest communication would not always be possible with our subjects, for reasons other than cultural conditioning and self-censorship. It took a great deal of time and effort to locate the subjects, and follow-up meetings were not always feasible. Usually no space was made available for us to have any private conversations with the subjects, as family members were invariably present in the congested living spaces, participating and often controlling the dialogue, and we had to try as hard to win their trust as to win the trust of the subjects. When we did manage to talk to them privately, there were time constraints and various kinds of disruptions. The issues of sexual choice and the larger questions of sexuality often remained sub-textual, tacit, circuitous, and we had to work intuitively, hoping and sometimes praying that our gestures and signals were being correctly decoded. Since the issues were not directly addressed, the solutions had also to be indirectly presented, in socially acceptable terms—a process that forced us to continually resort to subterfuge, invention, equivocation, deceit and actual lies, during our interventions.

We therefore found ourselves continually scrutinising our ethics, and as the work progressed we became aware that the documentation process was going to become more and more challenging. Since our efforts were not affirmed or mirrored by a supportive environment, our personal energy sometimes haemorrhaged away, and there were brief periods when from sheer exhaustion we silenced our own motivation to push forward with the work. In addition, we had to negotiate the demands of our regular jobs. We were always tense that our employers might find out about the project in some way, and we knew the response would be negative and phobic. On one occasion, when word somehow got to them that I was actively espousing lesbian causes, I was summoned and told to watch my step, since 'they' as an organisation would not like to be seen as supporters of 'such' issues. We were afraid of losing our jobs, afraid of being judged as individuals, and afraid that our associates would also be judged. On the few occasions when a friend or a subject with a sexually ambiguous appearance and mannerisms came to meet us at our workplace, it not being possible to meet elsewhere or at a later time, we actually had to request them to be more restrained in their behaviour, thus silencing them in the interest of self-protection.

But an unqualified belief in this project kept us going when our self-doubt was at its most intense. Negotiating the phobia of others as well as internal phobia catalysed a certain courage and nerve within us, and we attempted to silence the stares, sniggers and comments of co-workers by confronting them directly. The confrontation helped. Gradually it created a tenuous space for further discussion. Risking censure by our bosses, colleagues brought reports from regional newspapers to our notice. They even gave us contact information that might help us in locating subjects. But they told us, 'You will have to do the asking. We only know that people talk about them.' A colleague ensured that one of the 'talked-about' women—our subject Vimlesh—was invited for the workshop we were organising.

Vimlesh self-identified as male, completely and unhesitatingly. We exchanged addresses. One day I received a letter from her. I wrote back at once. She replied eagerly, and after we had exchanged some more letters I asked her if she would allow me to write her story. With quiet simplicity Vimlesh affirmed her attraction for women when we put the question to her. All the women in the factory that Vimlesh worked in knew about her sexual orientation. Later as we got to know Vimlesh better, we went to meet her girlfriend Kanak, who lived in another town. When we asked Kanak how she would describe her relationship with Vimlesh, she replied without hesitation, 'It is a love affair. I love her.' (The plural form of pronouns in Hindi create gender ambiguity, therefore Vimlesh's gender remained indeterminate in this form of address. But when Vimlesh referred to herself, she always used the masculine pronoun.)

Conversations with the partners of other subjects also provided us with crucial material for our narratives. Frequently, family members spoke for the subject, regardless of whether the subject was present or absent. In almost all the stories, the subjects have mentioned being aware of same-sex partnerships, and used the term 'women like me'.

The Stories

It is ironic that while our political intent was that of disclosure and revealing the intricacies of actual lives, we ended up having to consistently conceal the faces and identities of our subjects. Instead of speech/articulation, we found ourselves returning to various modes and layers and textures of personalised silence, within the wider, omniscient parameters of cultural/social/political silence around the taboo subject of female homosexuality. The experience of repeated circling back to silence compelled us to abandon our theories, discard our pre-existent judgements, alter the trajectory of our interrogation, scrutinise our actions, deconstruct our motives. We silenced ourselves, and we were also silenced literally and psychologically by our subjects as individuals, by their particular contexts and by the collective pressures of whatever social/community spaces they occupied. The censorship was self-imposed as well as externally imposed.

In the overall consciousness of the family/community/society/ state, the (homo)sexualised subject has no name, no face, no location, no body, no voice. How could we demonstrate that 'women like us' actually existed? We initially thought that women who had already been 'outed' by the media would be willing to talk about themselves. But we realised that it was going to be impossible to talk to the women even while we were able to meet them. Often the families stood in the way like the walls of a fortress within which the women were confined. But on one occasion we were able to meet one of the runaway women without family interference. Following up a newspaper report about a case of alleged lesbian elopement in Rajasthan, we were able to see how the nexus of denial operates from within the family right up to the state. Our first source of information about where the two runaways school-girls, Menaka (16) and Payal (15), lived came from the police. We were told the girls ran away because of poor examination results. The family said their daughter ran away with her friend because Payal felt unloved and uncared for by her stepmother.

What our fact-finding visits finally achieved was some perspective, albeit fragmented, on the aftermath of the disclosure, the denials and the difficult contexts within which subjects made their sexual choices. We clearly saw that a single exposure and a single headline rendered subjects even more vulnerable to various forms of policing, including drastic measures such as isolation, restriction of mobility, relocation and the pressure of immediate arranged marriage.

But during the fact-finding activity the interiority of our subjects remained elusive. The subjects were either unable to speak or un-willing to in the presence of family control. Paradoxically, our lack of success in this regard itself rendered the contours of our project more precisely visible. Whatever knowledge we gained of the situation and the subjects came through deduction and interpretation as well as pure intuition. All the stories clearly indicate the control that family and state exercise over women's sexuality. We also found that because these controls denied us access to the subjects within the home/private space, our efforts to access the subjects' thoughts and feelings often materialised in exterior settings—public spaces such as railway stations, terraces, ponds, parks, roads, etc.

Most of our subjects did not speak English and were equally unfamiliar with the words 'lesbian' and 'sanglaingik' (Hindi for 'same-sex'). Neither did they use a parallel, politicised term from any other language. In their own contexts, the male form of address and gender-ambiguous plural forms in Hindi was used both by the masculinised subjects and by people around them. The words used were Babu, Bhai. These are generic male forms of address. Most often the same-sex partners referred to each other as *dost, saheli, sathin, sakhi*—terms which, like the term 'female friendship' itself, are general in nature, non-threatening to the heterosexist paradigm, and socioculturally acceptable.

Using the term 'husband-wife' to describe homosexual partnership can be deceptive, because in practice these relationships are often egalitarian, negotiable and even transformative. Manjula, a married subject with a small child, and her partner Meeta, a separated woman, met at their workplace in the city. Manjula's husband lived in the village. Meeta had come to the city from her village to earn a livelihood after terminating her marriage. They began living together. Their friend Shobha, who introduced us to the couple, says, 'When I joined the unit as a Home Guard, Manjula and Meeta had already been there for two years. They were known as the 'miyan-bibi jodi'. They always reported for their duty together, Meeta riding a bicycle with Manjula sitting behind on the carrier.' Their choice of garments—Meeta always dressed like a man in trousers and shirt, while Manjula wore women's clothes—seemed to replicate stereotypical male-female gender coding.

It is interesting to notice what Manjula and Meeta agreed to disclose and what they would not speak about in terms of their personal lives. Though known as the 'husband-wife pair', unlike a traditional heterosexual couple they talk openly about the frictions in their relationship. In choosing the extent and the manner of their telling, easy and almost casual, they project an apparent transparency that skilfully deflects further interrogation. In the village they will not be allowed to live together as 'friends', but in the relative anonymity of a smaller city the partial visibility of their 'friendship' has protected them from social judgement and punishment. But the powerful force of denial that is imposed upon the women clearly has an equally powerful influence upon their relationship. Their narrative is open to interpretation at many levels.

Some subjects had resisted, to the best of their ability and under great strain, the almost intolerable familial/social/cultural pressures

of an arranged marriage. This refusal to be conditioned by traditional notions that marriage is a woman's desired, inevitable and
transformative destiny, is an assertion of selfhood that sometimes
results in the relationship being sustained alongside of or despite
the complexities of marriage and motherhood. This is illustrated
in the case of Razia and Sabo, from a village in Uttar Pradesh. They
had loved one another from childhood. But both were married off
against their wishes. Sabo, an activist who worked with us for
many years and came out at the time of the demonstration against
the ban on the film *Fire*, said, 'I did not have a choice, how many
women have a choice regarding marriage and having children?…
We had no idea that our friendship represented the possibility of
living differently, living with each other. All we knew was that we
did not want to marry.' Remaining committed to each other in spite
of their circumstances, Razia and Sabo have somehow, against all
odds, managed to integrate their relationship into the weave of
traditional marriage.

At many points during our interaction with the subjects, there
was an intense mutual discomfort at raising an issue directly connected with activities that heterosexist ideology and the heterosexist
environments we were negotiating consider illegitimate, perverted,
sinful, unutterable, and forever punishable. However there was no
such block when it came to us asking, or the subjects answering,
questions regarding emotional intimacy and friendship.[5] Keeping
the mainstream heterosexist response in mind, we asked ourselves
why it is that the somewhat nebulous, poetic category of 'female
friendship' instantly seems to become disreputable if it is termed
'homosexual', and almost repulsive when it is termed 'lesbian'. Is a
sexualised female friendship different from a lesbian relationship?
By giving something a different name, are we rendering it different?
What makes the term 'lesbian' distinctively political, while the term
'female friendship' remains neutral? Why is it considered dangerous—and dirty—to associate with a 'lesbian', and safe—and virtu-
ous—to associate with a 'female friend'? If one self-identifies as a
lesbian or is identified by others as one (and this image may not
coincide with what is imaged back when one faces the mirror),
exactly what is being interpreted, and to what extent? Is it one's
ideology, affiliation, activity, preference, practice, orientation, one's

essential selfhood or a subjectivity that is constructed of arbitrary signifiers? Is it a combination of these? Would the identity of 'female friend' be interpreted in the same way? Or would the general conclusion be that a 'lesbian' and a 'female friend' are altogether different species? Does the established, respectable frame of the second category effectively prevent the phobic gaze (both homosexual and heterosexual) from eliding it with the first? What, and whose, purpose is served through thus blurring the boundaries?

The gendered spaces and codes prescribed for women in the sociology of daily life excludes the visually more masculine/androgynous subjects, or renders them an ever-problematic and often shocking exception to the rule. From early childhood our subject Vimlesh had refused to feminise her boyish appearance. 'She would cut the frock with scissors whenever I made her wear one,' her mother had told us. All her life Vimlesh kept very short hair and dressed only in men's clothes. When we asked her how she dealt with phobic stares and derogatory comments in public, she bravely said, 'I am not bothered by other's people's opinions.' At another point in the interview, in the context of a question about her health, she said, 'I have to be very careful of what I eat. I can't eat this and that here and there, nor can I eat the rich food at weddings and such events.... In any case, I do not enjoy such occasions. Everyone tells me, go and sit with the men.... But apart from that, it is not my habit to go and simply chat, or gossip, or eat with people I don't know, I cannot just eat and drink with any and everyone unless we share some understanding. So I rarely socialise.' Vimlesh was initially aloof even when she talked to us. Her mother and sisters let us in more easily. But later it became apparent to us that her reserve was a habit, developed in response to the pressures of having to negotiate her complex situation completely on her own.

Vimlesh resists the binary division of male-female. She asks, '...Do bodies alone make us men and women? First we are not all that different when we are young...when my body began to change like all men and women's bodies do...I felt strange. Besides no one had prepared me for these changes, I did not know about these things. But I had to accept the law of nature. I thought, because of these changes I cannot stop living.' While recognising the socialisation that is imposed according to biological dictates, Vimlesh is choosing her sex/gender—wearing male clothes and in adamantly refusing to marry men. S/he demonstrates the flexibility between genders and the adoption or performance of roles beyond what s/he has been anatomically assigned. But such courageous perspectives invite social punishment, especially when sexual desire/autonomy, a male prerogative, is assumed by women. The paradox is that Vimlesh and masculinised others like her completely identify as male.

Any implicit suggestion, or explicit proof, that the homosocial space of female friendship is also potentially or in actuality homo-erotic, is also countered with immediate punishment. Sheila Sharma, one of the subjects we interviewed, was brought to our notice in the context of a tenant-landlord dispute. We found that the room had been let out to Sheila only after the complainant's daughter Lali had become friends with Sheila. When we finally met Shiela we told her that we had been to her village in Haryana and that we had a written statement from the people there, alleging that she lured and sold women. Sheila turned pale. We did not press her for details. Later when we asked her if she had ever been beaten, to verify the villagers' accounts of how she had been punished for eloping with a woman, her vehement denial convinced us that she did not want to share that segment of her story. We did not ask about the incident again.

We have to acknowledge the silence between the urban and rural contexts, between activists with class privilege and those from the working class, between our own varying levels of Westernisation and use of English, and the grassroots reality we were trying to understand in its own languages. The fact remains that the lives of most of our subjects are equally distant and alienated from upper-class, urban Indian as well as all Western representations of homo-sexuality, and their personal struggles, which cannot be separated from their socioeconomic struggles and traditional contexts, are largely unmirrored and therefore remain largely unknown.

Any mainstream/majority acknowledgement of sexual difference would naturally demand a critique and restructuring of established social powers and privileges. At the same time, marginalised sub-jects have no choice but to forge alliances with the mainstream, exploit similarities and alignments with the dominant group, in the interest of physical survival and psychological self-preservation.

The marginalised live in the mode of classic 'double consciousness' that characterises all minorities—the marginalised have in-depth understanding of themselves as well as of the dominant group, and apply this knowledge in order to survive on a daily basis, while the mainstream feels no need to develop a reciprocal understanding of the marginalised.

This lack of mutuality and the mainstream insistence on slotting the marginalised as a problematic 'other' (not an 'other' *with* problems but an 'other' who *is* in and of itself, existentially, a problem) is exemplified by the persistent political and socio-cultural silence, invisibility and absence conferred on lesbians in India. There are few autonomous, non-heterosexist relationship models and little or no thoughtful media coverage of homosexual issues. The media, to quote lesbian activist Ashwini Sukthankar, continues to rely on 'the discourse of catastrophe' and focuses on cases of same-sex elopement, suicide and other causes of public scandal. This reinforces the stereotype of the homosexual as tragic victim, and denies that the non-institutionalised relationships may in fact offer valuable alternative models of sexuality, family and community within the all-pervading culture of heterosexuality and its prescribed, gender-specific regimen centring around marriage.

Through our research and interviews, we have come to a tentative understanding of some ways in which our subjects resisted this patriarchal regimen. There were obvious contradictions in rhetoric and behaviour, for on one hand some subjects denied that they were in a same-sex relationship, but at the same time refused to marry, or if they were married, refused to make the marriage work. In most of the stories we documented, the subjects have had to separate from their lovers due to family pressures, lack of support and support structures, compulsory marriage or other obligations and coercions. Our subjects had no choice but to live out their various patterns of same-sex choice within patriarchal institutions and sociocultural ideologies supported by patriarchy—for instance, religious sects which accommodated female couples but also (presumably) imposed rules of celibacy. During a field visit to the pilgrim town of Vrindavan, we learnt of two women who lived together, one of them often dressed as Lord Krishna, as part of religious practice. When we tried to locate them we were told that one had left the sect; we found the house of the other woman empty. A boy who worked as the caretaker told us how upset this woman became when her partner left. She herself had departed the previous day on a pilgrimage. We also learnt that neither woman had ever been married.

Our subjects also skilfully used the patriarchally-sanctioned space of 'female friendship', since it was seen as non-sexual and therefore non-threatening. Often, socioeconomic necessity was in fact used as the rationale to live together, with both partners working—they shared living space, rent, finances and domestic responsibilities. Subjects also used traditional family structures to participate in one another's lives, sometimes to the extent of supporting each other's dependents and relatives. The more masculine subjects tended to consistently adopt male modes in order to create a space for themselves in a society where men are more privileged. Minturn and Kapoor (1993) describe a woman called 'Bhai' (brother; also used generally as a male term of address), a 'virgin widow'. Bhai always wore loose men's shirts as her upper garment. She married a widower on condition that the relationship would not be sexual; she would live with him and raise the children from his first wife. The men in the village respected Bhai to the extent that they allowed her to smoke hookah with them, a rare gesture of equality and acceptance.

One after the other, these stories remind us that in the midst of intersecting oppressions, each of our subjects is a political radical, a cultural rebel and a potential/actual agent for sexual autonomy and social change. We accept that the larger political, sociological and psychological questions we have raised through these stories, remain questions. But on some level the outcome of our interrogation is irrelevant. What is and always will be relevant for us are our subjects themselves, and women like them. In the face of overwhelming opposition and intractable circumstances, they have tried to realise their dreams. It is humbling to interact with such heroism, which will never be celebrated but instead battles daily with the constant threat of being disgraced, ostracised or even killed. These so-called ordinary, obscure, anonymous lives are in fact quite extraordinary. The phobic state and phobic society that combine to powerfully oppress such powerful spirits are finally the losers.

At the end of this project we find ourselves returning to silence—not from fear or censorship but from a feeling of awe, that irrespective of all the words exchanged and all the words left unsaid, the subtle pulse of a living connection, spun from itself like spider's silk, affirms that somehow, against impossible odds, some of us have actually reached each other.

Notes

1. Letter dated 10 November 1994, Ref Jag/94-95/10083, signed by the women in Jagori. Several women's groups wrote back expressing support, but the nature of the strategy adopted made that support relatively private and invisible.
2. Letter dated 20 February 2001, signed by Sehba Farooqui on behalf of the State Council of Delhi State Committee of NFIW.
3. Undated letter with the names of Kalindi Deshpande, Ashalata and several other individuals appended, but without their signatures.
4. UDHR Article 12.
5. Culturally sanctioned spaces for the expression of female friendships/bonding rituals have always existed in India and have a long history of being aesthetically imaged within the approved canon. Mythology, miniature paintings, temple carvings, lyrics of classical and folk genres of poetry and music, folk songs, stories, ceremonials, all provide rich variations of the figure of the *sakhi* or best friend, the *dasi* or faithful maidservant, confidante/attendant/witness who carries messages, brings good and bad news, arranges (strictly heterosexual) trysts, testifies to partings and unions, and shoulders the weight of the heroine's sorrow if love is unrequited, and rapture if the love is returned.

References

A Report: Fifth National Conference of Women's Movements, Tirupati, 23–26 January 1994.

A Report: Sixth National Conference of Women's Movements, Ranchi, 28–30 December 1996.

AIDS Bhedbhav Virodhi Andolan. *People Like Us*. New Delhi: Imprint, 1999.

Bhaiya, Abha (ed.). *Kinaron Pe Ugti Pehchan*. New Delhi: Raj Kamal Prakashan, 1996.

Caleri (Campaign for Lesbian Rights). *Khamosh! Emergency Jari Hai! Lesbian Emergence: A Citizens' Report*. New Delhi: 1999.

Dwivedi, A.N. and S.K. Sharma. *Holy Life of Narayan Mahaprabhu*. Allahabad: Kitab Mahal, 1996.

Gandhi, Nandita and Nandita Shah. *The Issues at Stake: Theory and Practice in the Contemporary Women's Movement in India*. New Delhi: Kali for Women, 1991.

Minturn, Leigh and Swaran Kapoor. *Sita's Daughters: Coming Out of Purdah*. New York: Oxford University Press, 1993.

Rothschild, Cynthia and Scott Long. *Written Out: How Sexuality is Used to Attack Women's Organizing*. San Francisco: International Gay and Lesbian Human Rights Commission and the Center for Women's Global Leadership, 2000.

Shri Nirmal Narayan Mahaprabhu. *Narayan Chitravali*. Allahabad: Jyotirupa Prakashan, 1999.

Sukthankar, Ashwini (ed.). *Facing the Mirror: Lesbian Writing from India*. New Delhi: Penguin India, 1999.

1

Guddi and Aasu

The month of January. A cold eruption of evening fog stretched like a white sheet in all directions. At the assigned time, we waited for our intermediary Pushpa, who lived in the same locality as our subject. Sniffling and shivering, we followed her to Guddi's house.

Guddi opened the door herself. A small bindi on her forehead, a necklace of white beads, two thick plaits swinging behind her shoulders, fists shoved in her coat pockets. Smiling, she said, 'Come in, how is it that you happen to visit? Whom do you wish to meet?' I was meeting Guddi for the first time, but out of respect for my age Pushpa was standing behind me. Now she thrust her head forward and said, 'She is like a sister to me. She wishes to meet you.'

Guddi opened the door wider. 'Come in, come in....' We stepped into a narrow room. Guddi's elder brother, a thin young man with wheatish complexion and heavy-lidded yellowish eyes, was sitting on the bed. Seeing us he rose, greeted us with a namaste and asked with some curiosity, 'Have you come to meet Guddi? I will go outside.'

He left the room, and Guddi promptly spread a *chatai* on the floor and moved towards the kitchen. 'Please sit, Didi, I will make tea.'

Pushpa said, 'No, please don't bother. It is so dark, who knows when the electricity will come. Just sit with us for a while.'

In Delhi's congested resettlement colonies the houses, no more than 20 yards each, adjoin each other wall to wall. There is not space enough to knock in a small window so that a ray of light may find its way in. In this atmosphere, even a crack of light shining from under a closed door would dazzle the eyes. At one end of the inner room was a long plank upon which were set *thali*s and pyramids of upturned *katori*s. In front of these utensils flickered a tiny one-rupee candle that alone was courageously battling the dense darkness. Guddi's *bindi* occasionally flashed in the glow. The tiny spray of sudden red scattered across our wandering, wavering shadows like the sequins in a *lehenga*.

Guddi clasped her knees, looked into our eyes, smiling. She said, 'Pushpa, at least introduce me! I have seen Didi around here....'

Pushpa was tall and lean, with brown eyes, her movements swift. Pushing her short hair behind her ears more out of habit than any real need, she fixed her gaze on Guddi, saying, 'Yes, you must have seen her. Her name is Shanti. Like me, she works in a women's rights organisation. When she heard about your case she wanted to meet you. Don't be afraid to speak. She also respects such relationships. Hence she came here. Answer her questions, and whatever help you and your friend need, specify that as well.'

I said, 'What is your age, what is your friend's name, how old is she? What is going on these days in your lives, can you describe some of that?'

Guddi replied, 'I am 19 and my friend Aasu is 21. She lives in the next house. We have known each other for five years. We would be living together openly today, had my mother not interfered. First of all, she forcibly got me married off. It has been one year since the marriage. But I only stayed in my in-laws' house for three months. On the first night itself I told my husband, "Until I give my consent do not try to initiate any physical relationship with me. If you try to force me, I will retaliate forcefully." He actually agreed to my conditions. We were getting along fairly well. Aasu would come to visit me. Then my family got to know that she was visiting me. My mother immediately arrived at my in-laws' place. Somehow, she made sure that they understood about us. She said, "If Aasu comes here, break her legs. She does not hesitate, she is coming to set your house on fire. For two years this girl has cast a spell on my daughter, worked some black magic. They are besotted with each other. If they don't see each other daily, they start running fevers. My three sons and I, we are very frustrated with this. I thought things would change after Guddi's marriage but this has not happened. If that Aasu keeps coming here, it will not be possible for my daughter to establish a household....'"

Hearing all this, Guddi's in-laws' attitude and behaviour towards her had changed. She became afraid that they would turn violent. She often began to wonder if they beat Aasu up, what would happen? When her husband began to force himself on her, she ran away from there. She said, 'I will not go back to my in-laws, no matter how much my family pressurises me. They constantly say, go back, go back. I have replied, I will go back on condition that Aasu comes with me. I will live with her only.'

'But,' Pushpa interrupted, 'Aasu is not supporting you in all this....'

'Who has told you she is not giving me her full support? People try to ensure that we are kept apart, but do you doubt our commitment? If we don't see each other daily, we don't eat. My house is next to hers, if we are not able to talk, we go up to the terrace and communicate through gestures. These days the atmosphere at home is not good. From the time I returned from my in-laws, everyone in the neighbourhood is making fun of us. They exclaim, "Two girls have set out to marry one another! What times have come to pass!" And they laugh and laugh. Everyone in our families, from youngsters to elders, watches us vigilantly and my older brother is always at home. He keeps such a strict eye...' In mid-sentence Guddi abruptly stopped.

Guddi's brother had silently entered the room. She was sitting with her back to the door so she had neither seen nor heard him. But somehow she had detected his presence. Over how many years must she have developed this instinct for self-preservation! Now she could almost sniff out approaching dangers, and had become an expert in preparing her defences instantly. We sat facing her, but before we could furtively signal to her she said, without changing her position, '...she works very hard.'

We immediately understood. Gathering up the ball of tangled threads Guddi had thrown towards us, Pushpa said, '*Bhaiyya*, please come and sit with us.'

Without letting the thread slacken, we said, 'Guddi was just mentioning you. Now that you are here, we would like to hear from you personally about your situation. What work do you do? How many members in the family, how do you make ends meet?'

The brother replied, 'My name is Pappi, that you must have come to know. We are three brothers and four sisters. Guddi is younger than the brothers and the other sisters are younger than Guddi. Our father is no more. Our mother sweeps and swabs floors in bungalows, to earn a living. Two brothers build and repair sofa sets. I don't go anywhere, I have a permanent ache in one leg. I've tried all kinds of treatments, hospitals, doctors, herbal, *hakimi* medication, where have I not gone, but nothing has helped. Now, defeated, I have given up. I am the eldest, and yet made helpless by my leg, I have sat down, and the other one who has sat down is this Guddi. She has caused us endless worry and tension. By now you must have heard all about it.'

Listening to him it became clear to us that the household was struggling to cope with daily expenses. Because of unsuccessful treatments, the young man could not contribute. Except for Pappi all the family members, minor and adult, work. Even so, the combined earnings amount to so little that the exactly-measured, minimum daily expenses cannot be met. Dealing with losses and illnesses, while continuing to abide by social laws, extracts a very heavy price from those who are economically powerless. How could we sit in judgement? To extricate one strand from this complex knot, and hold one person responsible or identify one reason for the family's many problems, was a dilemma for us. The laws of marriage between men and women are based on class, caste, religion, region, ethnicity and many other specific criteria. These constructed rationales are given the name of 'destiny' or 'nature', thus made to seem inevitable, unavoidable, normative and permanent. The traditional patriarchal forces that frame these laws are severely threatened by even the slightest suggestion, from any source, of an alternative or a change.

Under these pressures, the family got Guddi married off despite her repeated objections, after taking a loan at a high rate of interest. The burden of repaying the loan, along with the existing stigma of being a family headed by a single woman, was a double humiliation for the family. And now Guddi had returned home, destroying whatever effort had gone into ensuring her married status and gaining social respectability. As a result, there was a constant angry policing of her movements.

It was impossible to talk to her any further at this point. We lingered a while communicating through intent glances that we would contact her again. Then we had to take our leave. But even as we got up to go, Guddi became sullen and withdrawn. She was angry. As soon as we came out I commented, 'Guddi is angry. Why?' As we turned into the narrow lane outside the house, Pushpa replied, 'She does not know exactly when and how she will be able to talk to us. Come to my house, we can relax. I will tell you how I came to know about Aasu and Guddi.'

That evening, however, the darkness fell early and it was bitterly cold. The seeming impossibilities of Guddi's situation weighed on my mind. Besides, I had to return home to attend to various chores. I asked Pushpa if we could meet the next day. She agreed. We decided to plan a meeting where the issue of sexual preference could be discussed, so that some support could be garnered around the issue. We hoped the process would enable us to identify other women involved with women.

For one reason or another, however, we met only about three weeks later. That day the weather was equally bad—intense cold that sank into the marrow of one's bones, and no signs of sun. The ground was soaked with dew. Squelching through the mud, we reached Pushpa's locality.

Narrow lanes branched off from identical narrow lanes. It was impossible for an outsider to distinguish one tiny dwelling from the other. The last time we had visited it had been dark, but daylight was not helping us that day. Fatigue settled over us like the fog that enveloped this labyrinth, morning and evening. Then we saw a small child swaddled in woollens, watching us from the turn in the road. We asked, 'Where does Pushpa live?' Shoving his hands deeper into his pockets, he indicated the lane with his head. 'This is the way.'

Reaching Pushpa's house, we found a young woman sitting in the front room while Pushpa squatted and vigorously scrubbed utensils. 'Come, Didi, I was waiting for you.' She rose and rinsed her hands. 'This is Shalini. She lives in No. 20. She has two daughters, and she sends both to school,' she announced with pride. Pushpa introduced us and named the organisation we were representing. 'Shalini wants to talk about Guddi, so I invited her here amongst us today.'

She had barely finished her sentence when another woman entered, followed by three students, two boys and a girl. The youngsters busied themselves in a corner, the woman sat watching us. Pushpa quickly set some water on the stove for tea, saying, 'Didi, begin your questions, Shalini knows all about Guddi. These two boys have come to me for tuition, soon there will be a crowd of more children. We must make use of the time now.'

Somewhat hesitantly I said, 'Pushpa, you too are a member of an organisation. You were to tell me about Guddi, how you came to know about her. Why don't you go ahead, I am here to document all that happens in the meeting.'

Putting cups of tea into our hands, Pushpa said, 'Women from a community-based women's group came to our group, gave us Guddi's name and address and said, "You must be knowing her, she lives close by. Her husband came to us with his problems. He has been married to Guddi for one year but she does not wish to stay with him and has returned home. She will not go back to his house. He told us that he works and earns enough, and we have confirmed this. There is nothing objectionable about him. He is hoping that we will intervene and find out why she refuses to stay at her in-laws. He is hopeful that we can affect some kind of truce between them."

Pushpa and her colleagues from her organisation called Guddi over and talked to her in the presence of the community group. In front of them all Guddi declared that she did not want to go to her in-laws because Aasu was her intimate friend and she wanted to live with her.

The community group felt Pushpa must go to Guddi's house and convince her that she should abandon such childishness. They said, 'She is an adult, she is married, she should live responsibly. The sensible option is to leave her house, go to the in-laws and take up the work of running a domestic establishment. She has a decent husband. She should not ruin her good fortune with her own hands. She might regret her actions later.'

Pushpa and her colleagues assured these locality women that they would talk to Guddi and get her response. One fact was clear, that Guddi had not wished to be married. In such cases, no matter how decent the man, Pushpa felt that they could not put pressure on Guddi to get married. 'It is up to her, how can the woman submit? Indeed, why should she?'

Collecting the teacups, Pushpa continued, 'When we met Guddi she was filled with justifiable rage. She expressed her frustration with the interventions of the local group. We tried to explain that all women's groups are not similar. We urged her to talk frankly about herself. She was so angry, at first she was unwilling. But we persisted in contacting her several times. Once a connection was formed, she was ready to talk. She told us that when she had described her situation to the community group, initially they listened to her in complete silence. Then suddenly someone's repressed giggle escaped. Gradually all the women began to laugh together. "For them it was a joke, an opportunity to ridicule us, while for us it is a question of our lives," Guddi remarked furiously.'

'One of the women said in a puzzled manner, "If this practice becomes common, how will life be passed on?"'

'Another exclaimed, "What evil times have come, that these girls should be involved in such pursuits...."'

'A third philosophised, "This is just a temporary fixation, it will pass. Let it be for now."'

'A fourth concluded, "This is the result of giving girls freedom."'

Discussing it among themselves, the community group had decided that Guddi should go to her in-laws and Aasu must remain in her own house and not try to meet her friend. Otherwise Guddi would not be able to settle into that household. If Aasu was a true friend she would voluntarily distance herself after Guddi's marriage. Guddi should accept this.

Pushpa continued, 'When we met Guddi we told her that if she wanted to marry Aasu we would support her. But they have to be ready to deal with the day-to-day conflicts. Guddi said Aasu would make her decision after the marriage of her younger sister, for whom a proposal was being negotiated. If some scandalous gossip happened to be circulated the negotiations might be halted. So Aasu was waiting.'

Guddi was taking a big risk. Aasu may or may not keep her commitment to Guddi. But marriage was also not an answer. She had recognised her own desires and choices and now she wanted the right to live by them.

Shalini, deep in thought, said, 'Two girls cannot marry one another...they are only girls, where will they live? How will they find rent, food, clothing...?'

Pushpa countered, 'Your husband abandoned you years ago—are you not surviving, running your life? Aren't you feeding yourself, keeping a roof over your head?'

Shalini replied with some indignation, 'From the time my husband ran away with his brother's wife, I have raised and educated two daughters on my own. They have never gone to sleep hungry, I have earned for them and for myself. What I meant was, how will two young girls live? Society will not leave them alone. On top of that, jobs are so hard to find. I myself came here today to discuss that problem. If you know of possible work anywhere, please tell me.'

Unexpectedly, the woman who had come with the students said, 'I too have heard about this case. Guddi's mother-in-law has told the community that if Guddi does not return to her husband, Guddi's family will have to reimburse them for all the expenses the in-laws incurred during the marriage. They will not relent in this regard. You and I are ready to support the girls, they may be ready to fight with society, but from where will the two of them get so much money? How much time will it take? Just think, will the husband's family sit quiet all through it? What work can two girls do? Sweeping and swabbing and cleaning utensils can at the most bring in Rs 2,000 per month, if they work in several bungalows. How will they be able to stretch that money, to feed themselves as well as pay the debt? Also, talk about such relationships takes wing in all four directions. No one gives loans easily, especially to girls with a blemished reputation. Then how will they fulfil the payment? This case is also an issue of money...!'

Pushpa said, 'First of all, they have to commit to sharing a daily existence. Then our group will arrange for some basic supplies, so that they are at least able to live together.'

Shalini had been listening carefully. She said, 'I remember a case from my childhood. My village is near Moradabad. In our locality there were two girls who loved each other but both were forcibly married off by their families. Neither girl could adjust to her in-laws. There was continual tension and fighting. Ten days at the in-laws and then a month at their mothers' houses. The in-laws as well as the girls' families were really fed up. In the midst of all this one of the girls had a child. Eventually the family got tired of the struggle to dominate her, and left her alone. After returning home in this way the girls started living together. They lived at one edge of the village. One of them used to wear men's clothes. She drove a *taanga*. Without caring about people's opinions she used to steer the horse through the bazaar, to the railway station, everywhere. The other girl stayed at home. They stayed together all their lives. I don't know if they are alive today. They had great will to fight their families and society in such a forceful manner. If Guddi and Aasu show similar courage, let me know whenever they are in need, they have my support.'

Pushpa broke the silence that followed this narration by saying passionately, 'I am almost 20 years old. My brother, sister-in-law, neighbours are always demanding, "Why do you wear a pant and shirt? Wear salwar-kurta." I don't because I don't like to. They bring up the subject of marriage. I reject it. First of all, I will not marry. And if I live with someone, my companion will be a woman. I have an intimate friend, she is married but we meet, join each other in times of happiness and sorrow. Truly, we women survive through maintaining relationships with our chosen ones, with our parents, our communities, even with plants and trees, living creatures, mountains and rivers. We keep our bonds with all of nature, that is our enduring strength and our special skill.'

'Now take Guddi's mother for instance. Eventually she did not violate her daughter's wishes.' I looked up in surprise as Pushpa looked around and smiled broadly. I realised then that Guddi's story had contined to unravel in the last three weeks since I had met her, and why should it not. Looking straight at me, Pushpa continued, 'Shall I tell you what happened further with Guddi and Aasu? After we had met Guddi three or four times, her mother turned up here one day. She said, "Advise me what to do. The man is handsome, decent, employed, comes from a good family. And Guddi has returned from the in-laws after three months without letting him lay a hand on her. Even then he says, that it doesn't matter, and that he will wait. My mind is telling me, I should approach my younger daughter. If the man is acceptable to her and she is willing, I will discuss the possibility of her marriage to Guddi's husband."'

Exhausted and defeated, Guddi's mother had come to Pushpa after a day's hard labour to share this with her, and return home with some hope. Pushpa had stared after her, thinking that even if one searched far and wide, one would not be able to find such a mother. Had she wanted to, the old woman could have sent Guddi back to the husband. But she said instead, 'If my daughter does not wish to go, I do not wish to force her.'

Pushpa continued even as my eyes misted over at the thought that there might still be some hope for Guddi after all, 'This morning Guddi's mother came and sat for a while. I affectionately put my hand on her shoulder. "What happened?" I asked. "All is well, you must come, two days later the marriage is in the temple in the evening. I have not invited many people, perhaps 15. I will be sending my younger daughter to her in-laws," she replied. I asked her "Did you talk to Guddi?" The old woman nodded and said, "I told her that I was fixing a marriage between her younger sister and her husband, and that she should not create problems later. Guddi said that she had no objection."'

Pushpa sat among us with a faraway look in her eyes, 'Today, somewhat more openly than earlier, yet still somewhat cautiously, Guddi meets her friend, Aasu, who is waiting for her younger sister's marriage to take place.'

❖

2

Rekha and Dolly

On 8 September 2001, the national Hindi daily *Navbharat Times* carried a front-page story about two young women who ran away together from their homes in Indore on 1 September. They went to a place called Dahod in Gujarat, and got married to one another. From Dahod they went to Beas in Punjab and took shelter with the Radha Soami Satsang, a popular sect which accepts unmarried women as members. From here they were forcibly retrieved by the police after their families lodged a Missing Person's Report. They were returned to their respective homes in Indore on 7 September.[1]

Other than the women's first names, which had been changed to protect their identities, there were no markers that would help us in locating them. The story had been reported by a news agency. First we tried to get in touch with a women's group we knew in Indore, hoping that they could give us more specific details before we set out to try and reach the two women. But like us, the group was hard pressed for time. It took us four days to find the name and phone number of the journalist who had filed the story. When we spoke with him, he was more than willing to arrange for us to meet the women. At this time, the women were still in police custody. However, when we reached Indore on 14 September, we learnt that they had been released. The journalist in question, Akhilesh Awasthy, was the bureau chief of the local office of the news agency United News of India. He did not have the addresses of the women. We told him that in our fact-finding work we often contacted the police for information.

It had worked in several instances. It worked this time as well. When Akhilesh called the police station where the Missing Person's report had been lodged, we were given the addresses almost immediately.

The locality where the two women lived as neighbours is called Jawahar Nagar. Small houses of not more than 25 square yards lined the road. Shops, telephone booths, goats, hens, *charpais* straddling the drains outside open doorways, crowded clotheslines, all blurred any divisions that may be known to exist between different social classes. Jawahar Nagar was about six or seven kilometres from the railway station, a congested new encroachment creeping up on the indifferent old city of Indore. As I walked with Akhilesh along the very narrow lanes between the houses I noticed that we were under severe scrutiny. Our obviously middle-class appearance and the fact that we were complete strangers added to the suspicion that quietly smouldered there after the scandal of the two women running away from their neighbourhood. It had barely ended, and here we were, an unknown man and a woman, intruding. The collective gaze I felt upon me relentlessly proclaimed that this activity was not worthy of a respectable woman. I could almost have squeezed mistrust from the air. It was crucial that I accomplish what I had come to do before some unforeseen obstacle I could not negotiate was placed in my path.

Right at the corner of the row of houses was a small shop that perhaps met all the needs of the locality. It had an unbelievable mix of goods, from masalas and soaps to stationery. A young woman sat in the middle of it all, reading a book. Her cheerful face invited conversation. I asked, 'What is your name?' 'Maya,' she replied, looking straight into my eyes. 'Really! That is my name also!' I said. We both laughed at the coincidence, and with that sudden connection there was an unspoken bond. I asked her about the two young women, Rekha and Dolly. 'Yes, they both live here,' she replied, pointing to a woman in yellow garments staring at us from some feet away. 'Where she is standing, that is where Rekha lives. Two houses further is where Dolly lives. But she also stays in another house round the corner, you may find her there.'

'We will go and see Rekha,' we said. Maya shrugged, as if to say, do as you please.

We walked towards the woman in yellow. She backed away. Other women who had been peering at us with intense curiosity disappeared behind various thresholds. A short man in a dishevelled state, with a long shirt hanging over crumpled trousers, planted himself in front of us. He turned out to be Rekha's maternal uncle. With a look of open hostility, he asked, 'What do you want?'

'We want to meet Rekha,' we said.

'We will not allow it,' he replied. 'It is all over, the matter is ended. We don't want to meet anyone. As it is, it is all over the newspapers. Please go!'

Quickly Akhilesh said, 'She is from Delhi, from a women's rights group...Mahila Sudharak Samiti....' He gave this fictitious name on his own accord. 'Mahila Sudharak Samiti,' he repeated, and this time his tone had a ring of authority. The name he had conjured suggested that I would give the erring women a word of good advice and admonish them to conform to social codes. Little did he suspect that I was there to endorse the step they had taken.

The name of an organisation somehow caused the uncle to relent. 'Mahila Sudharak Samiti? In that case...' He moved aside and accompanied us further into the lane. On the right was a half-doorway that one had to stoop to enter. Four or five women and various children were clustered there. Akhilesh remained outside while the uncle led me through. As we approached the inner rooms I asked, 'Where is Rekha?'

He pointed to a tiny side room. 'She is there, having a bath.'

The door was half open. I saw a woman in petticoat and *kurta* sitting on her haunches, slowly washing the long hair that hung over her head all the way to the floor.

Raising my voice slightly I asked, 'Is this Rekha?'

She lifted the hair, piled it up, turned her head and looked at me. I wanted to tell her that I understood her, that I was here to support her. I smiled but she did not. Had I been in her position, I too would not have trusted a smile that came from someone accompanying an uncle who had ensured that the family's control over me was complete, and completely unrelenting. Since he had let me in fairly easily, I was not aware of the gravity and extent of the control at that moment. Conforming in our thought to some universal belief that family units of one man and one woman are the nucleus of 'normal' human care and love, we rarely interrogate them, rarely contest the artfully contrived institutions dependent on hetero-sexual paradigms and women's subservience within these param-eters. Rekha had transgressed the boundaries of the 'normal', hence she had forfeited her right to familial love and care. Looking away from me towards the floor, she began to pour water over her soapy hair. In that instant I experienced the familiar chokehold of impos-sibility, the impossibility of making connections with one like myself, in these hostile habitations occupied by hostile kin who call themselves family and claim to be on our side forever. My feet felt heavy as the uncle urged me on.

The rooms seemed arbitrarily built, added to the tight existing space as and when the need arose. The family had gathered in one room that was spotlessly clean, a bed against the wall. He pulled out a chair for me but I sat on the floor with the rest of the household: Rekha's mother, one unmarried sister and one married sister who had come from her in-laws. Also present were some staring children and one bent old paternal aunt who seemed crazed with anger. I was very tense, wondering how to phrase my ques-tions, knowing that I would not have a second chance.

As soon as I sat down the aunt said furiously, 'I gave many warnings, that so much contact between girls is not good. How often I said, why is this Dolly always here, morning and evening! Once earlier also Dolly has run off to Dahod with another girl, our relative.'

The uncle snapped back at her, 'Don't bring all that up, it is not relevant.' The aunt got up and hobbled out indignantly. He continued, 'We just want everyone to keep out of it. But Dolly is impossible. Now she has filed a police complaint against our family, a harassment charge that one of our children was teasing her about this event.'

It was clear that no one would be allowed to speak in the presence of the uncle. I asked, 'Where is Rekha's father?'

The uncle said, 'We are construction labourers, work is not continuously available. You see our house, it tells you what state we are in. This event has increased our money problems. Rekha's father was so upset by the scandal that while he was riding on a scooter behind his relative, he suffered a loss of concentration and was hit by a bus. He is in the hospital now. He has told me to deal with this matter in his absence.'

He turned to the women and said, 'Bring tea.'

The mother got up. She seemed agitated, but was totally silent all the while. As she left the room, Rekha entered. I had been told she was eighteen, perhaps she was younger. She had studied till Class IX. She was slim, with very dark circles under her eyes. She wore a dark blue salwar-kameez without a *dupatta*, head bound in a wet towel. She unwrapped it, lowered her neck to one side. Thick long hair swung down in a graceful arc. She started to dry it, flicking it with the towel. Water drops scattered around her. A certain defiance seemed to pervade her whole being as she stood within the circle of her keepers.

As Rekha came in, the uncle was saying, 'These two say they have got married.' The whole room sniggered. He looked at me as if expecting me to affirm his comment and join in the mockery. 'Tell me, can such a thing be possible?'

I asked myself again and again, why I had come to the house. The dialogue was not leading anywhere. The family was in full control. Had I been too optimistic, thinking the women would be able to talk freely? Why did I overlook the fact that their families might have taken charge? Somehow I had felt that since the two women had openly declared their relationship, they would talk to me openly. But having had their privacy and autonomy violated and censored by kin, by the media, the police and other authorities, they were forced back into the realm of silence, which became their mode of resistance, means of protection, dignity, even sanity. I felt anger rise within me.

Somewhat incautiously I asked, 'Why is it not possible? It is impossible only because you say so.'

Rekha and Dolly had wrenched open a door where none seemed to exist. Before it was slammed in my face I wanted to put my foot across the threshold, force a space of interaction, keep some possibility of communication alive. I quickly said, 'Unfortunately we think that such a thing is not possible. If you really think seriously about the issue, what do women get in return for marrying men? Keeping in mind what most women endure in their marriages, I am surprised more women do not do this sort of thing more often.

But I am curious to know why you lodged the Missing Person's Report. In a strict sense, nothing has actually been lost.'

The uncle said, 'We were worried about her. Also, from Dahod they fled to Punjab. They would not have returned. It violates our family honour when women run away.'

Someone called him from outside and he left the room. I said to Rekha, 'Please come and sit here.' She came and sat by me. By then the unmarried sister had brought tea. As we drank it I took advantage of the uncle's absence to ask Rekha in a low voice, 'Why did you make the phone call to your parents to tell them where you were? They would never have been able to locate you had you not called.' She answered in an equally low voice, 'Actually they already knew that we were in Dahod. We had hoped that if we informed them it would at least make them call off the police search.'

If the women were given the slightest agency, if they were considered autonomous subjects, the families might have stopped looking for them and left them to make their own decisions. But since women are treated as objects, they are merely commodities, property, possessions of their families. Commodities, property, possessions do not have free will. Rekha and Dolly had the audacity to assign themselves free will, appropriate it, create it where it was withheld: a criminal act that deserved punishment.

I was groping desperately for a solution, knowing it was impossible, knowing we could not talk, knowing she could not get away. What support could I give her? Sifting through a sense of mental chaos, I said insistently, 'You do not have to get married. What can you do to support yourself?'

Rekha said, 'I can do tailoring.' She went to a doorless cupboard draped with a curtain, brought out some sets of *salwar kameez*. I was amazed at the professional excellence of the work. She added, 'I stitched this also, what I am wearing'" The clothes she was wearing fitted her beautifully.

Here was a skill that could have brought her the independence she was seeking. For all I knew, this might have been part of her plan for a future with Dolly. Rekha seemed so proud and aware of her craft. How often I was struck by the irony that women are held back not because they do not have talent, but because they have it in abundant measure.

At this point the uncle returned. Quickly I said, 'If you have any problems, any need, if the police or reporters trouble you, get in touch with me, this is my address.' I took pen and paper from my bag and wrote it out. As the chit passed from my hand to Rekha's, the uncle strode forward and wrenched it from her. We had not heard him enter. Both she and I were taken aback at the violence of his action.

'That woman,' the uncle said angrily as he folded the slip and put it in the breast pocket of his shirt, 'Dolly has gone and filed a complaint against us. But I have done what I could to stop these policemen from pestering us.'

'Who complained and about what?' I asked wanting to be certain that I had heard right.

'It does not matter, I have taken full precaution. Dolly had filed a complaint with the police against us and our family. She also said she was not being allowed to meet Rekha.'

This angry statement reinforced my perception that it was utterly crucial for local groups to understand and support women who chose to live with one another. Our efforts as outsiders from another city were not adding up to anything. Local acknowledgement of the crisis and local strategies of intervention would have made all the difference.

Seeing that further attempts at communicating with either of them was impossible, I took my leave. I must have spent a sum total of an hour in the house. I wanted to sit longer, but I sensed that they were waiting for me to depart. I was both angry and sad that I could not extend my hand to Rekha and say, 'Let's go.'

I left wondering what purpose the visit had served. How can women be protected from family, secrecy, denial, conspiracy, lies spoken and unspoken, heard and unheard?

All this while, Akhilesh had been waiting in the lane outside. He suggested that I try and meet Dolly as well. I said that since the two families were so hostile to each other, if I had been seen emerging from Rekha's house by any member of Dolly's household before I tried to meet her, I would be interpreted as a troublemaker aggravating an already tense situation. But he was insistent and persuaded me. It seemed worth the effort, since I could see how difficult it would be to re-enter the locality under any pretext.

Dolly lived a few paces away. Waiting for me, Akhilesh had seen her roaming around there, keeping an eye on Rekha's, a house that she could not enter. I went up to the door of Dolly's house. A dark ghost of a woman with grey streaks in her hair was struggling to pull a gas cylinder across the threshold. She was emaciated, with sunken eyes. Her whole being carried the imprint of lifelong hardship she had somehow survived.

I said respectfully, 'What is your name?'

'I can't even remember it,' came the venomous reply.

Undeterred, I said, 'May I meet Dolly?'

'Why? It is all over the newspapers, can't you get your information from there? Besides, she is not home!'

Another woman, slightly bent, squinting at me with weak eyes, came shuffling out, visibly angered by my intrusive, persistent presence. 'What do you want?'

I explained that I was from a women's rights group in Delhi, and was following up the case. Even as I spoke I felt my resolve falter, her glare itself had defeated me.

'We don't want any of your kind here. Go away!'

Somewhat despondently I trudged back to the shop from where I had received directions to Rekha's house. The young girl who ran the shop greeted me. Trying to change my mood, I said, 'This is excellent, you are working and supporting yourself....'

'No, actually I am sitting here instead of my sister, she runs the shop. I only help. But I wish I had the chance to read and write and change my situation in life,' she replied. 'I too do not want to marry.'

'But I saw you reading when I first came here to ask the way,' I said.

'No,' she said. 'I was just pretending.'

Taken aback, I could only exclaim, 'Really!'

I stood talking to her for some time. The thin woman from outside Dolly's house came up and stood listening to us. 'She is Dolly's sister,' Maya said, and smiled. I sensed the two women were friends. 'Who was the other person who was telling me to go away?' I asked. 'Our mother,' said Dolly's sister. 'At one time even I used to run a shop,' she remarked suddenly. Then she turned and called Dolly's name several times. But Dolly did not emerge. I gave the young girl my address and said she could contact me if she felt it necessary. Somehow I felt she understood the dimensions of what had taken place in the locality, and the urgency of my mission.

I am still hoping to hear from her. And though I was unable to meet Dolly, some part of me was deeply moved by her refusal to see me. As long as anger beats with our hearts, there is hope.

Later, on my return almost two months later, we wrote a letter on behalf of our group to the sub-divisional officer asking him to ensure that the two women be allowed to meet with one another, as he had earlier recommended. He did not write back.

Note

1.   I later learnt from the Indore-based reporter who filed the story that he had been asked by the newspaper to also send photos of the two women. But fortunately these were not published, because the media was fully occupied in covering the terrorist attacks on the World Trade Centre in New York from 11 September onwards. I also learnt that the Indore sub-divisional officer had dismissed the case, saying that the women should be allowed to meet freely; they were legally adults, and since they had committed no crime, they could not be kept in police custody nor could the families restrict their meeting one another.

3
Vimlesh

'That is Taragarh.' Vimlesh raised her arm and pointed to the mountain, Ajmer's most famous landmark. 'The climb is steep, one can tell by just looking at it. But just look at the other hills.'

I followed the line of her blue shirtsleeve against the peak's rugged profile in the orange flood of sunset. By contrast, the inclines of the other slopes were so gentle, it seemed the earth had simply raised itself in pleasure. I turned, wanting to share my observations, but remained silent as Vimlesh lunged to retrieve her nephew who was racing towards the low parapet of the terrace. She shouted, then pleaded, to coax him back. As our eyes met she said, 'Look there, the green building is the special spot for Muslims. And that right over there is the samadhi of Prithviraj.'

I looked away into the distance. Maybe Vimlesh did not see what I saw in the silhouettes of the hills. At that instant I was able to fully understand that she was busy living her life, completely immersed in her family, home and work. I was the outsider, entering that life in order to write about it. And because we both loved women, certain common struggles in our separate lives created a sense of mutuality. But she would be the speaker, I the listener; she the author, I the scribe. For other reasons too, boundaries were automatically set—our differences in age, work, class, education—I was the older one greying and experienced, my work was confined to reading and writing, I had the benefits of higher wages and education—the list went on and on. While the notion of oneness persisted, it was actually like a stack of mould-saturated clothes, which appear to retain their separate layers yet disintegrate at the slightest touch.

However, I was not a total outsider, not a stranger. Beyond the parameters of established social logic, I was acknowledging the truth of women like Vimlesh, who stood out in the same manner that Taragarh was distinct from the surrounding slopes. On that Diwali evening, as I gazed at them, at her, I felt strangely humbled.

From the terrace we watched the houses light up, as though someone was reciting a mantra that caused one flame to touch a second, a second a third, and so on till the entire city was flickering. The atmosphere of profound serenity was somehow inviolate, despite the din of firecrackers erupting in the smoky sky, Vimlesh's unlit house disappeared into the moonless night of *amavasya*, even as the radiance of neighbouring household *diya*s and lights contested the dark.

Before I actually met Vimlesh the first time, it was her voice that drew my attention. Somewhere in the middle of introductions at a union workshop on women, gender and work, came a voice surprisingly loud for a woman. 'Vimlesh Pandit,' she said, and then jerkily supplied the name of her union and the place she came from. She is shy, I told myself and looked up. She had a crewcut. Her brown eyes were set in a round face with chubby cheeks. In trousers and a fullsleeved shirt she looked like a teenaged boy.

My first glimpse of her passed off without a hint that we would carry our meeting out of the workshop into our homes and hearts over the next two years. The first conversation that drew us together was about our common love for Rajasthan. I became more alert when she said she was single and free as a bird, and intended to remain so until the end of her days. 'I have a right to do what I want,' she said defiantly. And then one day a letter arrived from her. I wrote back at once, she replied, and after some more letters had been exchanged, I asked her if she would allow me to write her story. During this time, another friend of mine wanted to come to Rajasthan with me, so we decided to visit Vimlesh and her town during the Diwali holiday. I thought I would ask her the forbidden question then.

On the phone Vimlesh said, 'Diwali will be a good time to meet. On that day I'll return early from the factory.'

'You are going to work on Diwali?' I asked in amazement. 'You are not given a holiday? What time will you return home?'

'At four.'

I did not have her house number or the street name, only the name of the locality and within it the name of the clinic that was a landmark. 'Everyone knows it,' Vimlesh said, setting my doubts at rest. 'Immediately behind the clinic a road goes down towards the railway bridge. Just a few steps from the road, if you take my father Vishwanath Panditji's name, anyone will point out the house,' she explained in a resolute manner. After this I did not seek further clarification. 'We will meet then,' I said, ending the long distance call.

On the appointed day, we found the locality and after looking around for a while, found ourselves outside a phone booth, disoriented. A passing woman stopped. 'Are you searching for someone's house?'

'Yes.'

'Whose?' We told her. She said, 'I'll just ask and let you know.' She adjusted her slipping pallu and disappeared with swift steps into the lane directly ahead. We were left standing there. Just then a boy came up. He said, 'The house you are seeking, you have left it behind.'

We were puzzled as to how he could have known this. He said the woman we had asked had made inquiries and sent him to guide us. We followed him, overwhelmed by the cooperation that seemed to exist in these towns, unlike the indifference and anonymity of the cities we lived in. After a few minutes the boy stopped in front of a plot on which two buildings stood. One was fairly large, double storeyed, and five or six feet to its left was the other, a square elevated single room. Vimlesh emerged from it. Quickly she walked towards us. She took her hands out of her trouser pockets and greeted us with a namaste, smiling. 'Come, come,' she said, clearly happy to see us. I introduced my friend. 'Did you find the house easily?' she inquired.

'We did not need to ask, really. We went past the bridge but went too far ahead, but people themselves asked us where we had to go, and brought us here.'

'Yes, it could be so. The kind of people who assisted you are long-term residents of the colony. The ones who live closer around here are the sort who have recently acquired money—mostly *harijans* and *chamaars*. They think it is below their dignity to help anyone.

It is the government's fault—it has pampered these people and made them arrogant. Even our jobs now are being cut. More and more work is being reserved for these people. The government itself is being discriminatory.'

'How is the government discriminating?' I asked, 'By the same logic there should be no ration cards, since the rich say that working class are poor because they do not work hard, not because there are no jobs or because the people are not given adequate wages.'

'I always end up having arguments with you. But what you are saying is true too, caste and the economic differences between the rich and the poor are discriminatory.'

What a strange dilemma, that within our separate, fluctuating circumstances all of us sometimes experience ourselves as empowered, at other times powerless. Yet when we get the opportunity to affiliate ourselves with those we consider powerful, we tend to forget that other contexts render us disempowered. Vimlesh is from a brahmin family. She enjoys upper-caste privileges, yet she is a woman and because of this fact she will never be fully empowered as a citizen. This is familiar to her. But this is not all. She wears men's clothes only, without exception, and because of this she has endured social suspicion, scrutiny and phobia. Yet she is unable to empathise with those castes considered 'low' and treated with the same suspicion, scrutiny and phobia by the 'upper'.

We took off our shoes in the verandah of the main dwelling and were about to enter it when we saw an elderly man on the threshold of the smaller house. We greeted him with a namaste. 'My father,' said Vimlesh. He greeted us similarly and then returned inside. 'He has opened a shop in that building,' Vimlesh explained. 'He is the one who attends to it. Sometimes I help him on my day off. I get supplies, lift and carry…My father is my guru. Why do you bother to document my life, he is the one you should be writing about, he has really struggled.… He is originally from Farrukhabad district in UP. But he has lived here for so long, he identifies as a local.'

She told us that her father had a sister and two brothers, and that they were orphaned when very young. 'His sister also died. The community decided that the persons who took on the responsibility of bringing up the children could claim their inheritance. But the various male relatives were unwilling. One of the village elders took my father in. He grew up in that house. The family shifted to Ajmer. When my father was fourteen he left the house for good, without any money or idea of where to go. At the railway station he met an army colonel who was posted in Gwalior. This man heard the boy's story and took him along. He educated my father, got him employed in the army. For many years he worked in the military canteen. He kept sending money to his foster parents in Ajmer. He got married and started a family. He had lost the canteen job by then and a mountain of misfortunes fell on his head. He found work as a gardener, then as a labourer breaking stones, for quite some time. Later he managed to get a job as a senior guard in the roadways. My mother took in tailoring work....'

'We are five children—my sisters Disha and Geeta, two younger brothers Anil and Neeraj, and myself. My parents raised us with great difficulty. With equal difficulty they have managed to get my sisters married. But two months ago one of my sisters suddenly lost her husband. They had gone to a picnic spot close by. It began raining, though normally the weather is always dry. The bridge collapsed and my sister's husband was carried away in a flash flood and drowned. That day there were many houses whose doors did not open at all. There was simply no one left in the family to open them. My sister is now left with two sons and a new baby, a girl, she is just eight days old.'

We entered the main house and soon after Vimlesh introduced us to her mother. I found her mother compelling—tall, thin, wheat-complexioned, somewhat androgynous, her gait firm, her posture erect as an arrow. She asked us to sit on a high box-bed pushed against the wall, while she took the chair opposite, her feet up. On either side of her on the wall behind, two cupboards without doors faced us, filled with photo frames of family members, plastic flowers in a vase, combs, hair oil and various other bottles. Vimlesh's mother turned her gaze upon her other daughter Disha sitting on the floor, very still, her head covered with a saree pallu. She looked devastated. Her baby girl was fast asleep on her lap. The mother gently tried to coax her to return to her in-laws, trying to make her understand that if she did not go back, she would forfeit all her rights in her in-laws' house. 'You need their support, your parents will not always be here,' she reminded her. Turning to us, she added, 'I try to make Vimlesh see this as well, that there are some advantages to being married. But she will not listen, regarding this or anything else. Money does not stay in her hand.' Arranged on the wall were three plastic butterflies of differing sizes, 'Vimlesh brought those back from Delhi when she had gone there for a union workshop,' the mother complained. 'She also brought shoes for her nephew which turned out to be too small. She is always spending. We have let go now. From her childhood onwards she has been unique. If I dressed her in a frock she would cut it up with scissors. She would only wear pant-shirt. And now her niece is doing the same! Pant-shirt or jeans, that is all she will wear....'

'People always say it is a burden to have girls in the family. But I am glad to have girls. When a mother comes from work exhausted, the daughter will always bring tea and serve her. Very few sons are concerned about their parents in this way.'

The younger daughter Geeta sat upright and talked without hesitation. She had attractive features and chocolate brown eyes. She said that from the time Vimlesh began speaking as a child, she would say, 'I am a lawyer, my name is Sanjay. I have a bungalow on Kachehri Road. What is your relation to me? I keep people like you as servants! Take me to my grandmother, to my aunt.' She insisted on this, cried, screamed, 'I have studied in St Anselm's.' But the family did not know of any such school, in which case how could the little child have known? The child would say, 'I have completed a law degree; you don't have to educate me further. I won a major court case and the party who lost murdered me in my car, to take revenge. I was getting into the car when I was stabbed. I had earned a lot of money and had quite a bit with me in a suitcase. Definitely someone stole it.' One day the girls' father returned home and told Vimlesh, 'There is a huge crowd outside "your" bungalow; "your" grandmother has passed away.' Vimlesh had begun to cry and had run outside. With great difficulty the family had managed to get hold of her. After this Vimlesh's father called an *ojha* to cure her. The *ojha* had tied a thread on Vimlesh, and the family believed that slowly the spirit that was possessing her was exorcised.

The mother added, 'When my labour pains began at the time of Vimlesh's birth, we passed through Kachehri Road on the way to the hospital. Maybe Sanjay's soul at that instant entered into my womb.'

Vimlesh had been sitting at a distance from us in a chair in the middle of the room. From time to time she got up and went out to check on her shop in the other building. But as soon as her sister began describing the past-life incidents, she left the room.

Later, when I got the chance, I asked her about the memories of her past life. She said abruptly, 'I don't recall anything.' I did not bring up the subject again. Noticing this, her sister Geeta said, 'She is like this, it is her way. Look at her, notice how she sits alone, immersed in herself. She has been raised in this house with a lot of love. We don't impose any housework upon her. We feel she belongs in a better household, and through some karmic force she has entered ours. She is not really attached to us. She is very close to Munka, a co-worker in the factory. They are friends. For several years now Munka has been staying with her mother, she was thrown out by her in-laws, now her husband too is dead. Her brothers allowed her to stay, thinking their sister would take care of their aged mother. Vimlesh goes in and out of that house. She gets angry with us very often. Contradict her, and she flares up. At times her anger is indescribable.'

'Now our mother gets tired from looking after the house, doing all the cooking on her own, tending to the goat and cow, washing clothes and utensils. When we married sisters visit our home we help out. But for daily help only Vimlesh is here, when she is not in the factory. When Vimlesh takes up the chores, they are not properly done.

As we walked out into the courtyard, Geeta kept talking, 'When she washes clothes they remain dirty, she can't get stains off the floor when she swabs. Look behind you at all those utensils, if you ask Vimlesh to scrub them she will certainly do so, but some food particles will always remain stuck to them....'

I turned to look at the utensils piled beneath the tap, and my gaze moved beyond them to the guava and pomegranate trees, to the beds of cauliflower, green chili, tulsi and coriander. Above us, an infinite expanse of blue sky. On the other side of the courtyard was a thatched shed in which a cow and two goats were tethered. 'Being a brahmin, our father received these as gifts during *shraadh*,' Vimlesh explained as she joined us. Beyond the wall of the house, at a slight distance, narrow corroded steps descended to a pond. On the far side was a mango orchard. The tranquil setting seemed to belong to a bygone age. 'Your house is very nice,' I remarked.

'When anyone talks of selling it, I get upset,' Vimlesh said.

'With great difficulty we built this house, we worked on the construction with our own hands, like masons,' her sister added. 'Vimlesh is excellent at such work. Anything but housework! Send her on errands by cycle, by scooter.... She asked me if I wanted to sleep in her room during my stay here. I said, "Your room is not fit to be occupied! I won't come there till you have cleaned it up." The way she has flung the bed across the middle....'

'Did she clean up?' I asked.

'Yes, I was going to see how she has re-arranged it. We'll have to climb the stairs just before we turn to go on the terrace, on the landing...it is that bolted room.'

Vimlesh is the only member of the household who has her own room. On the right wall I saw a shelf with a *diya* and a portrait of the deity Kareli Mata. Daily, morning and evening, Vimlesh prayed to Mata Rani, and also kept *akhand* fasts during the *navratras*. During that time she remained barefoot, even when she goes to work. She had pushed the bed against the wall, to appease her sister. Opposite the bed was a window. On the upper floor of the house there was only this single room and the open terrace.

Having seen her room, we followed Vimlesh downstairs and returned to the room outside the kitchen. Vimlesh's mother said hesitantly, 'Can you help to find a job for my other daughter? I believe that in the railways they give compensatory employment to the surviving wife or an adult child of employees. Vimlesh's brother-in-law used to work in the railways, now that he is no more maybe Disha can get a compensatory job there....'

'The union in the factory where Vimlesh works has contacts in the railway union. These things are more easily done through union pressure. If Vimlesh takes up the matter, it might come through.'

'Everyone says it is difficult to get someone a job in this way,' Vimlesh commented. 'Specially now workers are being retrenched. Also, nobody cares enough to listen.'

'Yes, this is true. The government's hiring policies do not admit new entrants easily, but the railway union is still strong. The only problem is that the work she may get may not be the kind she would like to do. Women are put into the fourth category, there one has to fetch and carry for the bosses, move files from here to there, keep the water jug filled!'

'Work is work,' Vimlesh said firmly. 'One has to understand that while working one cannot enjoy the comforts of home. But in government jobs one gets leave, benefits, security, that is good. Private employers do all they can, to get the maximum out of the workers. For example, in the factory we have to stand for ten hours at a stretch. Actually we cannot even stand fully up right, we have to constantly bend at the waist. As the items come out of the machines, rows upon rows of biscuits, we have to pick them up and take them ahead to the production line and set them for packing. I am lucky that I can pick up a full load at one time, others can only manage half. During the process we can't put a foot in either direction, even for a second, to stretch our cramped muscles....'

'There are 11 co-workers in my section of the line—eight women, three men. The women stay together all the time. When the boss raised our salaries, the men got Rs 100 extra, the women Rs 50. So we decided not to accept the raise. The boss called me and asked for an explanation. I said, 'Take these rupees and give them to your daughters. Your female employees are not inferior to any man.' The boss had to listen because though he pays the women less, he needs us more, and can exploit us more. Often he gives us the heavy work of loading because he knows women do not waste time on the job. Last year there was a conflict over the bonus. He offered us 8 per cent, we demanded 10 per cent, nothing less. But in the middle of the night he absconded. We sat without work for a month, then the union contacted his business partner and got the factory re-started. We were desperate for work so we agreed that for two years we would not demand any bonus or a pay raise. Earlier, the overtime was fixed at Rs 14, now it is Rs 7, that is all. No holidays and no Sundays off, otherwise our pay is cut. If for some reason you take leave, that day's pay is cut....'

'In the past few years the world has changed so much, soon the poor will not even be able to breathe. You were asking me what my dreams were. My dream is that there should be no poverty in this world. Right or wrong, the rich keep finding means to become richer and no one interrogates them. Our boss closes down one unit here, opens one in another place. The product goes from here but the label has another address. Our factory is reported as a sick unit, loss-making. The other unit's quota is met through underpaid contract labour, and the bosses' profits multiply while the workers suffer. Our factory has 150 workers, 90 men and 60 women. Most of the packing is assigned to women. So women are constantly anxious that a machine may replace our manual work at any time.'

Vimlesh's mother added, 'Now it has become impossible to find work. I want all my children to be educated. My younger son is studying, and he also earns a little by singing in kirtan mandalis. Even if he finishes his schooling, is there any surety that he will get a job?'

'The advantage of a government job is that one cannot be hired and fired at will,' Vimlesh continued. 'The salary is all right, one gets holidays and everything follows a procedure. Now, if we fall ill or need hospitalisation, we can't depend on anyone except ourselves. I've had two accidents—one day I was on the scooter with my younger brother and a tempo hit us from the rear. I had to have stitches on my head. My brother was knocked unconscious. That day some divine power saved us. We had to pay all the medical expenses ourselves. When I was injured on the job I had to pay for a lot of treatment which the bosses would not recompense....The cost was one problem, the other was that from that time I have had a lot of gastrointestinal ailments. I was in bed for a long time, the medicines had side effects, I gained weight and my blood sugar became high. I have to be very careful what I eat. I can't eat this and that here and there, nor can I eat the rich food at weddings and such events.... In any case, I do not enjoy such occasions. Everyone tells me, go and sit with the men. But apart from that, it is not my habit to go and simply chat, nor eat with people I don't know, I cannot just eat and drink with any and everyone unless we share some understanding. So I rarely socialise.'

'Your sister was saying that you frequently go to Munka's house,' I remarked. 'Is she a good friend?'

'Yes, I go to her place. She has many worries. Her sisters-in-law and brothers make her do all the housework and won't help out...I try to help Munka in small ways. For example, when I go to the *mandi* to buy vegetables I also buy some for her, the wholesale vegetables are cheaper and it saves her the effort. When we decided not to accept the pitiful bonus at the factory, it was difficult for her, financially. I lent her Rs 300. We women help each other, but we don't let the men know. They think, Munka has no man, let's take advantage of her. They talk crudely and suggestively in front of her, but with me they are careful, they know I am tough and can match them word for word and blow for blow if need be...but I don't react with physical violence the way I used to. Earlier I was always fighting, but I have had enough of that now.'

'You say "earlier" as if you cannot understand what has brought about this change in you.'

'When I was young I was foolishly naive. Right from the time I can remember, injustices provoked a deep rage inside me.' Vimlesh put her hand over her heart to emphasise the 'I'. 'The first time I raised my hand, it was to hit my teacher when she brought a stick down upon me. I took the first blow, and the second, but the third time the stick descended, I grabbed it midway and resisted her.'

'Once I raised my hand, it was simple to raise it every time some thing happened. I would hit out every time I felt a wrong had been done. This incident which started it all happened in school. We had this plum tree in the school compound. The girls would throw stones at the branches laden with plums. One of the stones hit my friend's head. It started bleeding and would not stop. I went and simply cut off the branches to put an end, once and for in all, to the whole thing. The teacher demanded to know why I had cut down the tree. But I had not cut down the tree, only the branches. The teacher began to hit me. She did not see the point that a boy had been hit, he was bleeding, and in future more serious injuries could take place. I was angry. You have to change as you grow and engage with the world. The world forces you to change. It was not as though I was aggressive by nature, but I was forced to change.... I started getting into fights and more fights. I even had several cases brought against me, charges of violence. I was so hot headed. As if anger lay on the tip of my nose. Any occasion brought it out.'

'Flying kites, playing marbles with the boys…all of that lasted a short time. My father had to go out of town to earn a living. I was the oldest boy at home. I did all the outside work for the family. Cycling came easily to me. I liked it too, all that going out. That sense of responsibility changed my childhood.'

'I was born in 1976 and I started working when I was 15 years old…I could not focus on studies in school. I finished my 10th class privately and then started working…I knew I would have to do this kind of work, so what would further studies have achieved? So I started right away. After linking up with the union and learning about workers' rights, some things started to make sense. But not all unions are ethical. For example, the beedi workers' union that come up here had leaders who took money from the workers, saying we will get you plots of land, get you housing…to this day, not a single plot or house has materialised. When one joins the workforce, one starts to understand the real nature of the world….'

'These realisations changed me. Earlier I used to write songs. One day I tore them all up.'

'Why?'

'No specific reason.'

'But why, there must be a reason. Didn't you keep even one song?'

'No, I was angry that I couldn't find a page I had misplaced, and then suddenly it didn't matter whether one page was missing or the whole lot. I used to enjoy painting, but I have no time for that now.'

'Do you have time to arrange for us to meet Munka?'

'Now? It's a bit late,' Vimlesh said, glancing at the large dial of the man's watch on her wrist.

'Tomorrow, before we leave?'

'You said you also wanted to visit the Chishti *dargah*.'

'We'll take the later bus, that way we can accomplish both things.'

Geeta asked in surprise, 'Vimlesh, are you going to the Chishti *dargah* also?'

'Yes,' Vimlesh said. Turning to us she explained, 'Normally I don't go in, I stand outside when I take others there.'

'Why?'

'I don't like it. Muslims were the ones who caused the riots, that's why India was divided….'

I had hoped that Vimlesh would be sensitive to other marginalised groups, since she was so marginalised herself, in her being as well as in her identity. But like most of us from privileged majority sections, Vimlesh harboured stereotypical biases about the oppressed castes and Muslims. I could not resist asking, 'Do you really think riots are caused spontaneously by one community, or are riots deliberately made to happen? Who likes their daily life to be disrupted by this kind of fatal violence? Do workers want their factories to shut down? Didn't you as workers get the factory to run rather than allow it shut down? Ordinary people whose lives are at stake when riots take place, would they start trouble? Who benefits from these acts?'

'The leaders, employers...the bosses...I haven't really thought about it in this way. After listening to you, I am forced to think. You do give a different perspective to things....'

We had spent a lot of time talking about all kinds of things, and it had become clear that it would be difficult to get Vimlesh to talk about her friend Munka because Vimlesh was always surrounded by her family. We would have to talk to her outside the house. In our society there are few available private spaces other than homes. But for women homes are never private. Vimlesh had her own room, but her only truly private space was her mind and her body. I observed that even when she sat among us, she somehow kept herself apart. With her family she manifested a specific persona, often withdrawn, solitary, sometimes flaring into inexplicable rages. Remaining deliberately aloof and separate, she differed from the family by temperament as well as appearance and mode of dress.

At the *dargah* Vimlesh came right inside with us, though it was not her custom. Telling us to cover our heads, she tied a kerchief over her crewcut and began deftly guiding us through the crowds, even as people stared at her. She narrated the history of the mosque and how people of different faiths, from beggars to emperors, had come there without ceasing for centuries.

From the *dargah* we went to on to meet Munka. It was a beautiful day in March, almost spring. The mellow sunlight of departing winter was upon our backs as we entered the old, dilapidated house in need of repairs and whitewash. Five or six rooms opened off a central courtyard. Munka lived with her young son and her elderly infirm mother. The atmosphere should have been silent and melancholic. But Munka's sparkling set of even teeth, white as the hair on her mother's head, dispelled every bit of sadness that may have had reason to stay on in that space. Her laughter rang loud and free, wrinkling up the corners of her gentle eyes. In contrast, the saree and blouse she wore was of a pastel shade, in keeping with the dress code for widows.

And as for Vimlesh, observing her here one could not have guessed that she was reserved by nature. She kept in step with Munka's high spirits, busying herself with making tea and participating in the conversation. Munka's mother was bedridden, old and frail. She looked older than her 70 years. We sat with her in the room. As I praised the old architecture of the house, Vimlesh entered with tea and interrupted my commentary, 'Munka's mother will leave the house to her sons, because that is the custom,' she said in an ironic tone 'Even if the sons don't bother about her, and care is provided by only the daughter. Amma, who do you think will protect your daughter and provide for her, after you? Don't you think about this?'

'Beta, it is the sons who inherit,' Amma replied without hesitation.

It was obvious that Vimlesh had a special place in this household, a unique bond with this family. Nothing she said or did offended them.

'Then Munka will stay in my house, regardless of whether her brothers want to keep her or not,' Vimlesh said firmly. 'Everyone needs a place to lay their head.'

The way Vimlesh and Munka talked and laughed, the way they teased one another, put me in a quandary. It was rare to see such an open demonstration of love considered illicit and perverse by social norms. I wondered if Munka was indeed Vimlesh's special friend. After we left, I said to Vimlesh, 'In Munka's house you seemed so different, relaxed, joking....'

'Yes, I am different with her. She is special. I confide in her. But my life is empty, blank without colours....'

'What do you mean?'

We had reached the main road. It was somewhat depressing to hear the stoic Vimlesh speak this way. She raised her arm and hailed a three-wheeler, saying, 'It is time for you to go, when we meet again we will talk some more.'

Suddenly, abruptly, this initiating and terminating of dialogue, the persistent weight of unasked and unanswered questions within which we sensed further questions, a strange flailing about for reassuring certainties—it was difficult to assimilate the load of such emotion. I could not grasp it, and I was unwilling to depart in the midst of such ambivalence. But Vimlesh left me no option. Her demeanour did not indicate that she wanted to share anything further. Yet suppressed matters sometimes rise unpredictably to the surface in relation to an inner need. Vimlesh's sudden disclosures had unsettled us, and now came this sudden severing. The autoricksha driver was waiting impatiently. It was as if we were going according to some schedule pre-arranged by destiny. As we seated ourselves in the three-wheeler I said, 'Write to us.'

'Yes, and you also write.'

We did write to Vimlesh in the following months. In response, she wrote how she was faring, adding, 'I want to ask you one question. You have learnt so much about me, will you tell me something about yourself, because I have a full right to know. I hope you will tell me about yourself....'

I marvelled at Vimlesh's forthright clarity. What she was really asking for was a greater equality in the relationship. In telling her story and making her family accessible she had made herself vulnerable to us. In contrast, what she knew about me was my position in the union and my work but very little about my personal life. Also, I could see that through the letters she was asking me what she could not ask in person—she had found a way out to negotiate the inequalities between us. I wrote back that I would be only too glad to talk about myself. From then on letters became an important mode of articulating what was difficult to express face to face, or openly acknowledge in person.

I realised that to talk to Vimlesh privately the next time, we would have to extricate her from the family space. I also realised that I would not be able to ask her 'the question' on my own. I asked my colleague Sunita, a self-identified lesbian who had worked with me on various projects for several years, to accompany me. Both of us would have to talk about our own lives before we could ask Vimlesh about hers.

On our next visit, the household as always welcomed us affectionately. The opportunity to talk to Vimlesh alone presented itself when we were asked to have a meal, and we agreed. Almost the entire family dispersed to prepare the meal. We were in the room by ourselves for a moment and my friend said quickly, 'Let's step out and see the pond.' 'Yes,' I reiterated, 'let's do that.' Vimlesh agreed. We left the house, walked along the bank of the pond and entered to a mango orchard. Dense shade and deep silence, a corner of this earth woven by sunlight sifting and flickering through the leaves. We were about to sit down when Vimlesh said, 'Don't keep your back to that direction. It has a shrine dedicated to Tejaji Maharaj.'

We turned round. Carved deep into an arched stone slab on one side was a coiled snake with its hood raised and flared. Right across the middle was a proud rider with a regal moustache and a turban tied round his head.

'Whose statue is that?' I asked.

Vimlesh narrated the legend. Tejaji Maharaj is a widely worshipped folk hero in Rajasthan. Originally a poor herdsman, he valiantly fought the local king and won back the herds of cattle that the king had forcibly seized from the helpless population. On his way to fight the king, Tejaji rescued a snake from the top of a blazing tree. But the snake was furious at being rescued, for it saw this death as its only salvation from the karmic cycle, and Tejaji had unknowingly disrupted the process. It cursed Tejaji, saying it could now die only after biting him. Tejaji promised to return after defeating the king and retrieving the herds. He came back victorious, but so badly wounded that his entire body was profusely bleeding. There was not an inch of unbroken flesh available for the snake to sink its fangs. Tejaji opened his mouth. The snake bit the warrior on the tongue and then died.

'Snakes are symbolic of sex and sexual desire, but it is a motif which has come to denote only male-female desire,' I remarked. 'And this does not hold true for all people.'

'Yes, it is not mine,' my friend said, 'Neither is it yours.'

'Yes,' I agreed, 'Vimlesh, tell me, what is your truth? Who do you desire, is it Munka?'

A slight gust caressed the mango leaves. As they quivered, Vimlesh said with quiet simplicity, 'No, there is someone else. She lives in another town. Munka knows about her. All the women in the factory know.' So easily she said it, without ado. And how long it had taken us to ask!

'Know what?' I persisted.

'That I desire a woman.'

'Don't people comment, stare at you the way they did when we went to the *dargah*, they were staring at you....'

'In the factory no one mocks me to my face. I am not bothered by others' opinions. Everyone has the right to eat what they want, wear what they want, live as they choose. From the beginning, I have dressed in this way, like a man. And I have always preferred women. Why it is so, I have never thought about too deeply. But it is not important to have an answer to everything. You ask if I have heard the word "lesbian". No, I have not heard it. Till you explained it to me, I had not heard any controversy about the film *Fire*, nor have I seen it. I consider myself a male. I am attracted to women. Why create categories, such deep differences between male and female? Only our bodies make us different. We are all human beings, aren't we?'

'Bodies make us men and women,' I said.

'Is that so? Tell me something, do bodies alone make us men and women? First of all, we are not that different when we are young.... When my body began to change like all men and women's bodies do, I felt strange. I did not like it. Besides, no one had prepared me for these changes. I did not know about these things. But I had to accept the law of nature. I thought, because of these changes I cannot stop living. I had to overcome the shock, adjust to these new developments in my body. But I hate the life of a girl. If I could, I would ask Brahma why he made me a female in body. If it was within my control, I would change my body just as I have chosen to wear men's clothes. When a human being is born, he does not know anything. He is told, "These are your parents, sisters, father and brothers". Similarly we are told, "You are boys, and you are girls". But I say I am a man. I choose to be one. Despite our physical differences, we can be who we want to be and do what we want to do. You are the one who told us, in the workshop on women, gender and work, that the tasks given to men and women should not be based on gender alone but on their capabilities and choices. All men and women cannot do all kinds of work. Different men and women can do different kinds of work. But the final analysis, we are all the same, we are all human beings, we are all equal, regardless of what kind of bodies we have. This common factor should be considered, not the ways in which we are different. This is what I said before, and I repeat it again.'

'In school I was part of a close group. In the Class VI one girl told me she was attracted to me. But at that time my thinking did not extend to such matters. This girl always wanted to be my partner when we played house-house and so on, but I did not take it seriously. At one point a cousin of mine, we call her Baby, came to visit from Aligarh, she told me about Jyoti, a friend of hers. We discussed such things. My brother too is aware of all this. A neighbour's daughter used to send me letters through him. I have met several women who are attracted to women, but I understood the full implications of this in depth only after seeing Jyoti at Baby's marriage....'

'Our family went to Aligarh for the ceremony. There I met Jyoti. That encounter was a bit strange. The wedding was to be held in the house. Crowds of relatives, dholak, music, songs, *mehendi*, clothes and make-up, food—it was a festive atmosphere. I was standing below the stairs when I saw Jyoti. As soon as my eye fell on her, I recognised something, some deep bond, though I was seeing her for the first time. I stepped forward and said, "Are you looking for Baby? She is upstairs." Jyoti pushed her way through us and raced up the stairs, declaring loudly, "These city people have no manners!"... Somehow I knew she had intended to connect with me. Baby must have told her something about me. I could hear Jyoti asking, "Where is Vimlesh?" and Baby answering, "She is down-stairs, you just now passed her."'

'During that wedding we kept encountering each other. When she was not present, I couldn't concentrate on anything, when she was around I always felt happy. Baby teased me, saying I had fallen in love. Looking at Jyoti, something was aroused in my soul. We both fell in love. I expressed my feelings to her. But we actually met very little. She was in Aligarh, I was in Ajmer.... We wrote letters. This mode of our relationship carried on for two years. Now it is almost seven years since we last met. A year after Baby's marriage, she too got married. For a while I kept meeting her.'

'Her husband did not like it at all....One day we were sitting on the bed, chatting and joking. Suddenly her husband gave her a hard slap. I was enraged, but what could I do? I stopped meeting her, stopped writing. The one I love, why should she suffer on account of me? My love always demands sacrifice. Nothing physical took place between us. We desired one another, that was where it stayed, to sit and talk, holding hands and hugging one another. We felt so close to one another.'

'To this day, I am pure. Sometimes I think I will take a vow of celibacy or become a renunciate, give up all attachments.'

'Is that possible?'

'What else can I do?'

'Who is this girl you have mentioned?'

'Kanak teaches children in a school in Bharatpur. My sister..."
Vimlesh stopped in mid-sentence. 'Listen, that is my brother calling. They must be waiting for us at home, it is time for the meal. We should go.'

We returned to the house, washed our hands and sat down to eat in the kitchen. Sparkling thalis were stacked with hot, perfectly round puffed-up fried *puris*, there were big *katoris* of potato curry sprinkled with chopped *dhania* leaves, and thick creamy *kheer*.

After this, the only chance we got to speak to Vimlesh in private was the next day, when she came to see us off at the railway station. In the deafening clamour and confusion of the crowded platform, Vimlesh told us that Kanak was the daughter of Vimlesh's sister's elder brother-in-law.

'We met for the first time at my sister's marriage. From the initial glance onwards, I really liked her. But that is where things stayed. After that, we were not able to meet for three years. Once we started to meet, her father objected. The hostility was not so obvious but he made it clear that he did not like my coming and going in their house. Her mother partly knows something, and partly pretends she knows nothing. Somewhere, she consents to our relationship. It is something that is merely tolerated, not entirely accepted. You see what I mean. I will introduce you to Kanak some day. You can also meet her on your own. These days she is angry with me. I went to Bharatpur for some work and returned without meeting her. Now she is studying for her MA exams. We can meet her together.'

It was time for the train to leave. We promised to write, and to finalise a date to go to Bharatpur with Vimlesh. However, busy with other work, we could not immediately follow this up. Vimlesh wrote more than once, inquiring how we were, adding, 'Do you not have time to write two words? I wait for your letter. Is it possible that you have forgotten me? It very often is the case that friendship is not possible between people of different classes, and if such friendship does develop, it is rarely sustained for long.'

We wrote back immediately, asking her to arrange a meeting with Kanak in Bharatpur.

On the way Vimlesh talked more easily, definitely happy to be with us. She walked with her hands in her pocket, her stride confident as she stopped to ask the way to Kanak's house, 'It is a rented house, not their own. I have been there only once since they shifted here. Kanak has another sister. There are two daughters. The younger one had also shown interest in me, but I was keen only on Kanak. Kanak's father now says, "What is the point of owning a house, when my girls go to their husbands' houses, who will be left here to take care of my property?"...'

'Do you think Kanak will get married?'

'What does my opinion matter? Kanak's father will not agree to any other arrangement. Kanak should at least prepare herself for it mentally. I have not thought that far. She has turned down many proposals. She says she does not want to marry. But when I call her to my sister's house here in Bharatpur, she will not come. She doesn't want to agitate her parents.'

'Would your parents, brothers and sisters accept your living with a woman into the house?'

'To conform to society, they will raise objections. But internally they will accept my choice.'

'Are you sure?'

'Well! They do understand I am different. But to this day I have not asked Kanak what she wishes. We desire one another but we have not even touched.'

'Never touched? But one always wants to touch the person one loves, knowing that perhaps they wish the same....Have you expressed your feelings to her?'

'She knows.'

Asking the way, we negotiated the locality and reached Kanak's house. It was big, with two-room units rented out to various tenants. The door was open. Kanak was standing by a tree in the long courtyard. She was tall, slim, fair, dressed in a polyester *salwar-kameez*, her *dupatta* neatly folded over her shoulders. She appeared to be the same age as Vimlesh. A long plait swung below her waist, moving in rhythm with her neck as she turned to Vimlesh and clapped her hands with a scream of delight. Vimlesh's face lit up. Then Kanak exclaimed angrily, 'I don't want to talk to you! Why didn't you visit me the last time you were here?' She was not in the least disconcerted by my unfamiliar presence. Vimlesh stood by happily. She introduced me as '*Didi* from our union.'

Hearing voices, Kanak's younger sister Raj came out of a room and her mother stared out of an adjacent kitchen. The daughters resembled their mother, who looked young enough to be the oldest sister. Both of them emerged and warmly welcomed us inside the house. Vimlesh had somehow found out that Kanak's father was not at home at that time, and that later he would be on night duty. Greetings, introductions and laughter filled the courtyard. We entered the living area and sat down on the floor, refusing the chairs. In front of us, on a high bed, lay various bundles and boxes. Madhuri Dixit sang on a small black and white television. Items of daily use filled the open cupboards. Raj went to make tea. Kanak's mother sat close to us.

'I can't believe it,' Kanak said. 'Had you come a little while later, we would not have met. How lucky we are! Raj and I were going to someone's birthday celebration. Now you are here, I don't want to go. I won't go.'

'Go after some time,' urged the mother.

'We will see.' Kanak often broke into English as she spoke. Later Vimlesh told me that she was taking special tuitions to become fluent in English. Looking at us, she said, 'You have dinner with us. Vimlesh can sleep here.'

'No, I'll go back to my brother-in-law's house,' Vimlesh said. Kanak tried to insist but with a determined shake of her head, Vimlesh made a clear gesture of refusal.

Kanak went to the kitchen to bring the tea. Seeing there was one cup less on the tray, I asked, 'Who is not having tea? You, Vimlesh?'

'I only want a little tea. We do not need two cups. One cup is sufficient for both of us.'

She took a few sips and slid the cup towards Kanak, who lifted it and took a big sip. We were still drinking the tea when Kanak's father entered the house. He was tall and well-built, wheatish complexioned, his right hand swathed in a bandage. Kanak's mother had told us that he worked as a mechanic in the state roadways. During repairs, a windshield had fallen on him. The wound was deep. The doctor had advised stitches, but he was afraid to have it done.

Kanak went back into the kitchen. 'I'll prepare food, you all must eat before you go.' After a few minutes Vimlesh followed her. Kanak's father sat down. He wanted to know where I worked. When he learnt I worked in a union, he warmed towards me. He was himself a union representative in his workplace.

'I have raised my daughters as if they were sons,' he said. 'Educated them well, these times demand it. My girls are fortunate that we give them full freedom. Both want to do post-graduation. Kanak is preparing for her second MA degree and she is also learning English. As regards education, we don't object to any of their efforts. We have agreed that they can take up teaching jobs in schools. Kanak teaches children for a few hours a day, that is good....'

'According to our social customs, both daughters are of marriageable age—but the prospective grooms have to be worthy.' In Rajasthan, to educate daughters properly and let them work, as was the case in this household, is unusual. Most girls are not that lucky. Kanak's mother herself was married at 16. Maybe that experience gave her the courage to resist social pressures regarding her daughters, even while acknowledging the reality of the system.

After a while Kanak's father left for his night duty. 'He eats only when he returns from his shift,' said the mother. Vimlesh came into the room and said to us, 'Come, let's go up. Bring your camera, you can take our photos.' As we climbed the stairs to the terrace, she added, 'She has my photo but I do not have hers. Take her picture and send it to me.'

On the terrace I squinted at them through the lens while they adjusted themselves into a pose against the parapet, close together, smiling. Vimlesh put her arm around Kanak's shoulders. Kanak pulled away. Vimlesh glanced at me and said, 'Did you see that? What were you asking me earlier? Can anyone do anything?'

Kanak quietly slipped her fingers into Vimlesh's hand and said, 'Yes, now take our photo.'

Face half-hidden behind the camera as I adjusted the focus, I said, 'Kanak, how would you describe your relationship with Vimlesh?'

As I pressed the button she replied without hesitation, 'A love affair. I love her.'

I walked to the far side of the terrace and left them together. After about fifteen minutes, when they had finished talking, we went downstairs. So long as we participate in silencing our own desires we will have to live off stolen moments, brief trysts on terraces, in one another's eyes, in dreams, between this town and that town, our visions shrinking like the stubby and shapeless noon shadows at our feet.

We returned to Delhi that evening. A few months later Vimlesh came to the city on union work. When we met she seemed happy and more at ease. She wanted to know how I was. After sharing some events of my own life, I asked, 'How are things with you and Kanak, is there any progress?'

'Yes, there is some progress. This time when I went to Bharatpur I went to meet her. We kissed and embraced. But we could not say or do more, we were both so embarrassed, it happened so suddenly. It was our first time. I thought my heart would split, I just got up and left. I was trembling. Later we talked on the phone. I cannot understand it. Earlier, as is normal with her, she expressed love without restraint. My sister, Kanak and I were in a three-wheeler, her arms were interlinked with mine, she was talking freely, openly, even with my sister present. We were eating food at home, she took a barfi, bit off a piece and put it in my mouth. I don't know how, she actually came to my brother-in-law's house to see me on her own. When I said, "I am sleeping alone in that room," she came along with me.... We lay side by side all night, talking. She says, "I have done your share of studying as well! Don't be tense about the future, you do not need to study." She says, "I will elope with you." On February 14 she sent me a Valentine card....'

'I don't know where this is going. The next time I am with her I will surely confront her, ask her what she wants, what she is thinking....'

Three months later we got a letter from Vimlesh. Kanak was engaged to be married, she informed us. After she got the news, Vimlesh went to see Kanak, who refused to meet her. Vimlesh tried to phone her but Kanak would not respond. 'If only she had spoken to me once, I would have understood. She owed it to me, to us, our friendship....'

Only when I began to reply did I realise the difficulty of the task, composing something that might be comforting as well as useful. But I was aware that my rhetoric was a mere patchwork of support at a distance, and redundant in the face of the enormity of events that had over taken Vimlesh's life. Just when she had begun to hope! What could I say that would make it better, bearable? I tried to remind her that in all likelihood Kanak had been forced into agreeing to marry. I reminded her that Kanak had resisted the pressure for a long time. I repeated what I had told her earlier, that it was time they frankly discussed their mutual expectations. I suggested to Vimlesh that she write to Kanak. I assured her that we were willing to give whatever support was needed. Should the need to leave her home arise, we would support that too. Later when I called, I learnt that Vimlesh had lost her factory job on account of her union activism. She was not well. Her father too was ailing. She wrote to me saying she had written twice to Kanak but had got no response. 'I want to die, my life is meaningless, no job, no money, nothing. I am angry with you also. You said you would come but you did not, I got the message you had called. I hoped you would call again. I want to talk with you. You are the only one with whom I can share what's going on inside me. The oppression, the suffocation, is killing me....'

I called back. She told me Kanak had called her, but they were not able to talk because Vimlesh was not home. 'You are right,'

Vimlesh said, 'She is not happy with the decision. I want to meet her. But I do not want to go their house alone. If you come, we can both go. Will you come?'

'Yes,' I said.

A few days later we met in Bharatpur. I called Kanak at the school where she worked. Vimlesh stood quietly beside me.

Kanak's voice sounded small and forlorn. 'Please bring Vimlesh. I have to see her.'

'I will bring her.'

As I put the phone down Vimlesh asked, 'What did she say?'

'She wants to see you. Her father is on night duty,' I said.

'Good.'

On the way to Kanak's house Vimlesh said, 'Please do not insist I eat anything or drink tea there.' I remembered what Vimlesh had said about being able to eat with only those people with whom she had some understanding. This was her expression of hurt and anger.

Kanak's family had shifted to a new house—a bigger one with more rooms. Their living space was on the first floor. As we climbed the stairs, I called out to Kanak. Raj and their mother came to the stairs. Kanak was washing utensils at the far end of the terrace. I preceded Vimlesh and was ushered first towards the room. When we turned to go in, Kanak came from behind and held Vimlesh in a close hug, completely hiding her face in Vimlesh's chest. While the three of us stood pretending normalcy, Kanak simply would not let Vimlesh go. Her mother urged me to move. This was a hug deeper than a meeting of two friends. Its trajectory encompassed forbidden territory. Perhaps that was why her mother was propelling me more urgently forward.

I asked myself, why is Kanak marrying? As I walked inside the room I saw a huge carton holding a television set, the first sign of dowry a girl carries to her in-laws' house. Kanak's mother followed my gaze 'Some things I have bought now, others we will buy later. Sit, please. You have to come for the wedding.'

I thought of Vimlesh, Kanak and innumerable others who stand on shaky ground long, long before their life even begins. Though Kanak longed for Vimlesh, she relinquished her dream in order to maintain family honour. She had won for herself the label of a 'good' woman. She had even freed herself of the certain struggle and danger she would have had to negotiate daily had she opted to live with the woman she loved. I sat there dumbly, barely able to muster a smile in response to being invited to the wedding.

Vimlesh walked in slowly a few minutes later. Too casual, I thought as I looked at her. Her face was calm.

'Where is Kanak?'

'She is coming.'

When Kanak's mother got up to make tea. Vimlesh said, 'We have to go. We will not have tea.'

'Don't go right away,' Kanak said as she walked in. She looked thinner and darker. We exchanged greetings and she looked away, blinking back her tears. When the tea was brought in, Vimlesh picked up her cup and put it on the window ledge behind, while making polite remarks. Kanak looked at me in desperate appeal. 'She will not drink it.'

Raj was telling me about the boy Kanak was marrying. Kanak and Vimlesh got up and went out on the balcony. I could hear them whispering as I sipped tea.

A little later Vimlesh returned to the room. 'Are we ready to leave?'

'Yes.'

We said goodbye. Kanak did not come down to see us off. As soon as we were alone, I asked, 'Well, what did she say? Why is she getting married?'

'She said that if I had come to her with the proposal before March, that is, before she got engaged, something could have been worked out.... But she also said that women have no choice. "My parents said yes to the boy's family, if I said no...where would it take my parents, family. It cannot work for us if we go against the wishes of our parents." These are her words.'

Vimlesh shared her sense of anger and betrayal in the letters she wrote to me, vowing that she would break off all contact with Kanak. But when we met several months after Kanak's marriage, she said Kanak had called. 'What was I to do? There are so many women but it is her I love. Maybe I should not have talked with her. I am angry with her. But I talked to her. What could I do? She has told her husband about us. She even told him she loves me.

He has asked me to come over. But I do not want to see him, nor hear about him. Before her marriage Kanak was loudly proclaiming our love, and then in the end she withdrew. What can one do? I am telling you, though I do not tell anyone at all, I am missing her.' Looking away, Vimlesh said in anguish, 'I wish she were here with me, sitting right beside me. I know there is no point in such thinking, and yet....'

'She tells me she has fantasies of running away with me. I told her she would have to give up the man she has married, her family, her sister mother, father.... Perhaps I too will have to sever my ties with my family. She said she is willing to let go of her family and husband, but that I would have to accept the life that she was carrying in her body, part of her bones and flesh...But I do not want the child! Why should it even come into this world? You ask why, what can I say? Such distances and such longing!'

'I did what I have never done before, I went to the *dargah* and bowed my head in that Court of the Almighty. I asked Him to give her to me. Before she withdrew from me the whole world seemed so wonderful, and now nothing seems worth living for. Thoughts of her fill my being, and it causes me so much pain.

'We cannot love anyone just anyone. If only we knew why we love the ones we do, perhaps it would be easier to find someone else to love. Before Kanak there have been several other women but it was not possible to reciprocate....'

"Even now, a month ago, I met a woman. I had gone to my sister's house in Jodhpur. This woman lives above my sister's place. She openly told me she loves me. She is married and has one small child. Her husband works in the cloth mill. He often has to work the night shift. When we were all going together to see the new park that has been created in the town, she told me she loves me as we walked together a little behind the others. I just kept quiet. Later in the night when I went up on the terrace to sleep, she was there. She approached me saying that she had lost her heart to me. I asked her what she meant. She answered rather seriously that what she had said was an expression of what she truly felt for me. I could not think of anything to say to her.'

'Then it began to drizzle and the raindrops were enough reason for me to get away without really answering her. "You will get wet,"

I told her, as I folded the cot. This is how I ended the conversation. In the morning she tried to talk to me again.... But all I could think of then and right now is Kanak.'

After the rain that day, two summers later, a small patch of blue led up to a full sky. Vimlesh's window in the shop opened on to a potter's household and in the wet earth behind the potter's wheel Vimlesh found an answering echo of her longing in the eyes of the woman who stood beside her father helping him knead and prepare the clay.

4
Menaka and Payal

In late May 1999, two schoolgirls, Menaka (16) and Payal (15), ran away from Alwar to Ajmer because they wanted to live together. The police were alerted by the respective families and the girls, spotted when they were changing hotels, were picked up by the police and returned home. The case was reported in a national Hindi daily. By now this plot, with its predictable ending, had become familiar to us but as we planned our fact-finding trip we were not under any illusion that our work was going to be easy.

Several weeks later, we managed to take two days' leave from our regular jobs, not knowing if this was sufficient time, or what to expect. However, we had learnt that often plunging into a volatile situation yielded better results than the most carefully thought-out plans. Also, we were committed to offering emotional support to those in such circumstances, even if we were unable to assist them in any practical way or bring about any change in the attitudes of their keepers.

It was a bright evening, with a cloudy sky in which the sun still shone, and a cool breeze. On the bus journey we prepared our strategy, wondering how to best reach the girls—whether to go to their homes, to the school, or to the police station. After discussing various possibilities, we resolved to arrive at a final decision only on reaching the town. We stayed overnight with my relatives, who welcomed us and asked us the purpose of our visit. As usual, it was a struggle to answer but we were practised in such evasion. We told them we were doing some gender sensitisation work among school-children.

We woke the next morning to the intoxicating smell of wet earth as the first monsoon showers fell. My relatives suggested that we wait a little while before venturing out because the locality we would be going into was sure to be waterlogged. But at 8 a.m. the sun miraculously broke through and it was as if it had never rained at all. Buoyed by the good weather, we stepped out to begin our search.

The girls' school was in a congested lane in the older part of town. At the gate of the school we found out that the morning shift was only for the primary section. We knew that the girls we wanted to speak to were in the secondary section. We also knew that the principal of the school came in at 11 a.m. Taking this into account, we tried to rethink our strategy. How would we be able to identify the two girls from amongst the hundreds in the compound? Even if we won the principal's trust, there was no guarantee that she would allow us, two unknown women, to meet her students. We also suspected that by now, two months after the incident, the families of the girls would be fiercely protective of them, perhaps the girls were no longer allowed to attend school. What if one girl had passed the Class X exams and the other hadn't—would we have to look for them among students from Class XI as well? What if there were several sections of each class—where should we begin?

The task seemed overwhelming. We thought the best alternative would be to visit the girls in their homes, but we didn't have their exact addresses, only information about the general locality, and we had their fathers' names and knew where they worked. How would we be able to find them in this area, not exactly the size of a palm?

Just next to a nearby temple was a shop selling buttermilk and curd. On impulse we thought we would ask there, since both the girls' fathers were brahmins. Pundit—temple—milk products: the ridiculous logic of this combination was our only dim hope. We approached and asked for the addresses of the two families. The shopkeeper, himself a plump pundit with a tuft, said with some curiosity, 'Give me some more information. Which place do they belong to?' 'Here,' we said foolishly, not able to answer any other way. He shrugged. We looked around and noticed the fortified medieval gate of the old town, upon which an arrow indicated the direction of the police station. Not really wanting to, but not having any choice, we walked towards it. We knew from the news reports of the incident that the First Information Report had been filed at this police station.

As we proceeded, I asked my colleague, 'What exactly shall we tell them?'

'We'll tell them the truth,' she replied firmly. 'That's it.'

'But how will we justify our presence in relation to the case?' I persisted uneasily.

'We'll say that we are from a women's group that works with runaway girls.'

After so many instances of having to lie, the decision to negotiate a situation without subterfuge left me almost euphoric, as the burden of secrecy fell away. We took a rickshaw to the police station. Inside there was a crowd of men, none in uniform. When we asked for the SHO (Station House Officer) we were ushered into a small room. Within a few minutes a man in plainclothes entered and sat down in front of us. Uniform shirts, belts, undershirts and trousers hung on nails in the wall, and were spread across tables and the backs of chairs. Clearly the room was also used as a sleeping area.

The SHO asked who we were. My colleague said, 'I believe you were a great help in solving the case of two runaway girls of this area, two months ago. Today we are here to seek your help. We are following up the case, on behalf of our organisation which is committed to fighting social evils. We want to tell these girls that the world is full of dangerous monsters who can destroy innocent lives. There was an incident in Orissa, where two girls who were close friends poisoned themselves....'

The SHO gave no indication that he had heard of the case, so we did not elaborate on it. This was the case of two young women, Mamta and Monalisa, who loved one another dearly and were known to be inseparable. Both women knew that their same-sex relationship was not acceptable to their families, and had filed an affidavit for a partnership deed so that they could live together. The imminent job transfer of Monalisa's father, a government employee, led the women to attempt suicide because they knew that they would be separated. They consumed insecticide and also slashed their wrists. Discovered while still alive, they were taken to the hospital. Monalisa died on the way, while Mamta survived and was later forced to undergo psychiatric treatment. While Mamta's father denied that the attempt to commit suicide was because of same-sex love, Monalisa's grandfather stated explicitly, 'It is a case of lesbianism.' In their joint suicide note the lovers had expressed the wish to be cremated on the same pyre.

My colleague continued, 'It seems to be a trend now, so many young women are running away from home. In such cases, we go and intervene.' The idea was to go on talking with him and break down his resistance. He was our only possible source of information. Fortunately, so far he was responding to whatever we were saying. We knew from experience it was a good sign.

'Whatever you may claim, madam,' the SHO said, 'we cannot reveal the addresses of these two girls. Do you have your organisation's card?'

We fumbled in our bag and pulled it out. 'Here, satisfy yourself. Believe us; we are genuinely supportive when such incidents occur. But if you hear of any other such cases, do let us know,' we persisted.

'Madam, this case was not about eloping with boys. These girls ran away because of their poor examination results. We know exactly why they behaved in this manner. They are back home and all is well. The trouble is that many people come from the press and TV to publicise the happenings, so the families object to our telling anyone where they live.'

'Please do not worry in this regard,' we said. 'This will never reach the press.'

The SHO sent two constables to escort us to Menaka's house. We followed them through the crowded lanes to a big *haveli*, with a small door frame and double doors. The building enclosed a central courtyard. We climbed up dark narrow stairs where we had to grope our way forward to reach the second floor. The constables knocked on the door and waited. A woman opened the door. They said, 'These women want to meet you.' We smiled and did *namaste*. Seeing the uniforms, she gestured to us to enter. The policemen left. We walked in. A young man who was later introduced as Menaka's elder brother Yash was sleeping on a *takhat* below the window. It was only 10 a.m. but the room was dark because the glass window panes had been covered with newspaper. The brother worked at night so he usually slept during the day, the woman explained. As we sat down, he woke and stared at us. We explained that we were from a women's organisation and described our work with women and families, and our efforts at intervention in unusual circumstances.

The mother brought tea. She was dark, short, and had an open expression on her face. One could see the resemblance between mother and son. Both listened to us intently. We said, 'We learnt that the girls ran away because they wanted to live together.' The mother replied quickly, 'It wasn't the way it has been explained. They were not worried about exam results. The trouble is that my daughter has a very soft heart. Anyone who tells her a sob story steals her heart. Payal has a stepmother, and she feels the stepmother does not care for her, she feels unloved. She wanted to escape from that woman. In their innocence, she and my daughter ran away together. Payal provided the money. When they were shifting from one hotel to the other the police spotted them, we had lodged a report that they were missing.... We all loved Payal. She came to our house each day, Menaka and she used to go to school together. She is just like a boy, can't stay at home, she knows how to drive a scooter, how to get around. We had no idea things would come to this.'

Yash added emphatically, 'We are not rich, if we had been rich and our girl had run off and returned even after four months, it wouldn't have made any difference. But for poor people, honour is the only wealth we have. My mother used to work as a school teacher, my father is a government employee. We are ordinary salaried class people. The mud slinging which will go on.... Our sister is not involved with any boy. Nor is there any problem within the house that would have compelled her to run away. Yes, it is true that our father is stern and dominating...but Menaka would not run away for that reason....'

'Where is Menaka?' we asked.

'She is doing puja,' he replied. Just then she entered the room. Dressed in a *salwar kameez*, she looked about 15. She was tall, lean and fair-skinned with a long plait, stooped shoulders and a down-cast gaze. Yet her whole body was tense with anger and her eyes were wet. We patted her head and stroked her cheeks with concern and affection. As the brother talked, Menaka sat rigid, her resistant posture indicating that she did not subscribe to his account.

He continued, 'The other thing that troubled us about the incident was the publicity. We had to face people we did not want to talk to. And we had to beg those very same people to stop spreading rumours. One magazine that publishes "True Stories" wanted to write about this incident as a dramatic event. To make things worse, in the news reports it is being said that Payal's family is blaming our family for what happened.'

We said to Yash, 'Well, despite whatever has happened, we hope you won't stop Menaka from completing her education—it is the only way out. Life is very difficult today if one is not educated.' It was clear to us that Menaka was not attending school, as it was July and the session had already started. Her mother had said she had not started to go to school.

We asked Menaka gently, 'What exactly made you take this drastic step of running away?'

She looked up and looked away, remaining silent.

We also sat silent, desperate to somehow communicate to her that we had come to affirm her action, not to add to its denial and negation. Then we said to the mother, 'Even if they did run away out of friendship and love, that is okay. After all, it is love, not hate, that makes them want to be with each other.'

The mother looked at us mutely, bewildered. Walking the tight-rope between mother and daughter, we asked, 'Menaka, what were you thinking, did you have any idea about how you would survive once Payal's money finished, did you consider how dangerous the world is for women in general, more so for youngsters like you both?'

'More people need to tell the young what you are saying,' the mother remarked.

Menaka continued to sit rigidly, in stubborn silence and obvious anger, eyes downcast. Somehow we had to reach her, make her see that we had come to support her and not her oppressors. Changing my tone, I added, 'We understand how friends feel for one another. Perhaps I might want to do it too. It is a good personal value, no doubt, but often one has to think through things before taking such a step. Maybe you could have waited for some time?'

But Menaka did not meet my gaze. Her mother muttered, 'She has learnt the lesson of her life. She is not prone to do such things...not her. She does listen to what we say.'

'Where does Payal live? We would like to meet her,' we said.

Yash willingly gave us the address and tried to explain landmarks that would help us find the house. He told us that in all probability we would not meet any of the family since Payal's mother went to teach in a school and the father too would have left for work at this hour. Yash called his younger brother Ankit from another room and instructed him to walk us to the point closest to the Payal's house. From there we would have to proceed on our own, for Payal's family should not find out that Menaka's relatives had revealed the location of their house to outsiders.

'Have lunch with us, then go,' the mother said. We thanked her for her gracious offer, however refusing it and took our leave, saying that we had several other tasks to finish during our short time in the city. Menaka continued to sit rigid and frozen. She did not trust us. When her mother walked to the door to see us off, she got up too. I thought she looked less angry. She stood behind her mother, and without a nod or wave, smiled very slightly. Perhaps she understood that we were on her side and committed to offering her support.

We followed Ankit through various congested lanes in the bazaar. From the top of the lane where Payal lived, he pointed out the house. We walked up and pressed the bell. Immediately a curtain was pulled aside from a window in the house opposite, and a woman stared at us curiously through the mesh. We got a sense of being perceived as intruders, and became slightly nervous—maybe the press had been here too, and we were being associated with them. We were afraid our presence might re-aggravate the scandal.

However, the door was suddenly opened by a young girl. 'Payal?' I inquired with a smile. 'Yes,' she said, not smiling back. She had short hair, light eyes and features that expressed some inherent sense of happiness. But she also seemed wary and not particularly welcoming. We entered and suddenly realised that she was alone in the house. It was a great relief to not have to invent a reason for our presence. Quickly, aware that our time was very limited, we told her we belonged to a group working specifically on sexuality issues.

'We read about you in the newspapers,' we said. 'After coming here, we spoke to Menaka's family. They say you ran away because of your stepmother.'

'How is Menaka?' she asked at once. 'I keep calling her but no one answers the phone and she does not call me.'

'Her family seems to be controlling her,' we said. 'They also said your family is blaming them for what happened.'

'I hope Menaka understands that all this is just to keep us away from one another,' she said. Then in a sudden change of tone that showed how completely in charge she was of herself, she added, 'No, it was not because of my stepmother or the exam results or whatever else people may say. We loved one another and we wanted to live together. What options do we have but to run away. It was not going to be possible for us to live together. Our families would never agree. We had hoped no one would find us.'

We had been unprepared for the sheer good fortune of finding Payal alone in the house; and now we were equally unprepared for the actual utterance we had wanted to hear, and which came so effortlessly from her: that she and Menaka ran away together for reasons of love.

'How did you think you would support yourselves?'

'I would have taken up any job that came my way. We would have managed.'

We said, 'When you take steps like this without thinking it through, you see what it comes to. It is not feasible....' We stopped, aware that the words were brutal. We were also aware of Payal's anger. And we understood it fully. It was almost as if what we were suggesting—that she consider all the odds and only then take such a step was a further criticism and effort to subjugate the freedom she had claimed with great difficulty and at great personal cost.

Her mistrust became obvious when she said bluntly, 'You were talking about a group in Delhi. Is there any such group here?'

We replied, 'We don't know about a group here, but we know local women's groups, we can put you in touch with them, if you need help of any kind.'

She seemed disinclined. We also told her she could keep in touch with us. We exchanged phone numbers. 'When you call, identify yourself as Pooja,' she warned.

We assured her we would stay in touch. There was so much to say, now that she had spoken the truth. But it was past noon and her stepmother was expected back at any moment. All our conversation had been hurried and furtive, contrary to the need Payal had expressed—the need for a group where she could meet with others like herself. We recognised her need. It was not so many years ago that we too had yearned for such contact. We knew that awful pain of isolation and the sheer weight of the storm that has no answering echo.

We would have liked to have sent Payal reading material and letters, but knew these would in all probability be intercepted. During the next few weeks we only managed to talk to her twice on the phone; at other times family members answered the call and told us she was not at home. The two conversations we did manage to have were brief and tense. Clearly she could not talk openly or for long. Ironically, she kept asking about Menaka, so it was clear that the families had succeeded in keeping the girls apart.

We returned to the town three months later, and first went to Payal's house. As we approached, through an open window we saw a man inside. He gave us a strange look and intimidated, we left without trying to contact her. We then visited Menaka and her family, and they received us affectionately. This time too Menaka's father was not home. The mother sat with us and talked while Yash stayed around for a short time before he left for work in the evening.

Menaka was there, more cheerful than when we had last met. She told us about her wish to become an Air Force pilot, and that she wanted to study with that goal in mind. We talked about many things, including whether it was possible for her to be friends with Payal. For Menaka's family the crisis had obviously blown over. The mother said, 'Payal's family is still blaming us for the whole incident. I don't think friendship is possible.'

We kept in touch with Menaka over the phone, but after a few months we began to get taped messages from the exchange stating that the number was out of order. Concerned, we soon made a follow-up visit. Everything looked the same, the familiar courtyard, the familiar narrow, dark stairs. No one answered our knocking. A staring neighbour suggested we knock louder. We did. Ankit, the younger son, who had guided us to Payal's house on our first visit, opened the door. As we stepped in, we saw that the whole house had changed. The neat, orderly look was gone, furniture upon which we had sat the previous times was also gone, the shuttered window had been opened and a stream of intolerable sunlight poured through. The flustered Ankit kept asking us to sit down. Half blinded, we stepped further into the room, now partitioned by a steel almirah. The spotless kitchen had disappeared, and the rubber pipe was hanging out of the nozzle of the gas cylinder next to dust-laden cooking vessels stacked forlornly in a mesh basket.

'My father had an accident a year ago, after that he couldn't climb the stairs, so the family has moved to our own house, far from here, it is across the town,' Ankit explained. 'I work as a videographer, I run my business from here. Three months after the accident my brother Yash had a court marriage to a girl he liked, against my parents' wishes, and went away to Chandigarh....'

'Yash?' we exclaimed, surprised that he, with his traditional notions of family honour, had personally gone against it.

'My mother was supposed to have an operation but it did not take place because of these upheavals. Yash has returned now and we are reconciled.'

It was all part of the same structure that oppressed Menaka—while her transgression was prohibited, policed and punished, Yash's act was negotiated; not only that, he was forgiven and accepted back into the fold.

'How is Menaka?' we asked. 'Is she studying?'

'Yes, but she is completing her studies privately. After my father's accident she had to stay home to look after him, so she could not give the science exam. Now she is in Class XII, doing arts. My mother and family will be very happy to meet you.' Ankit gave us the address and we left with a heavy feeling. The family had endured many misfortunes. And the one story that never changes across many towns is of the girl/woman who must give up her dreams and commit herself to family duties.

We found the house after some effort, late in the evening. We asked the autorickshaw driver to wait. The family was surprised to see us, but welcomed us warmly. The father had been severely injured while returning from the bank. He had hit his head against a construction rod and fallen unconscious. While he was in this state he was run over by a jeep. Some people took him to the hospital. During surgery metal rods were put into his thigh to support the shattered bones. He found it very difficult to walk. He had also suffered memory loss, and at times was not able to recognise his family or relatives. He seemed cheerful enough, however. He could no longer continue his work as a clerk in the municipality, and was due to retire the following year. Menaka came in after a few minutes, wearing a T-shirt and long skirt, hair plaited, *mehendi* fading on her palms. She told us she was studying history, political science and sociology. 'I want to become something,' she said firmly. She had acquired a new set of friends with whom she went to school. She didn't talk much, only answered questions briefly. Yash's wife, nineteen and pregnant, sat in a corner with her sari *pallu* covering her head. She looked like a child.

Menaka's mother tutored neighbours' children and ran a small sweet shop in the front room. Children came in and out to pick sweets from glass jars lined up on the window sill. 'It keeps me busy, and brings in Rs 40–50 each day,' she explained. The room had a bed and a TV. A narrow passage connected it to the inner room and the kitchen. Stairs led to the terrace. We went up. All the terraces were linked by common walls. One could hop from one terrace to the next, all the way down the lane. The family planned to build two more rooms upstairs for Yash and his wife. Menaka's mother had bought the 45-square-yard plot from the local development authority 13 years ago. The total cost was Rs 25,000, being paid in instalments of Rs 207 per month, she explained after we returned downstairs.

'A wise decision,' we said, admiring her resolve and foresight. 'I wish I had bought two such plots, they were so cheap thirteen years ago. Now they are all occupied by different people.'

There is a stretch of open ground in front of the house; the neighbours had asked Menaka's *pundit* father to take charge of building a temple there. He had collected Rs 14,000, and hoped to collect about Rs 30,000 more. 'I would like to start the construction soon,' he said. 'But after this Ayodhya-*kaand*, we've been told to go slow, to do everything quietly and gradually.'

'Why not build a school instead?' we asked.

'The children here don't want to study, they are not interested in reading and writing. They won't come.'

'Do you meet Payal?' we asked Menaka.

She lowered her gaze and said in a soft voice, 'No. She is not a good person.'

'Why?'

'She spread all kinds of lies about me, about my character....'

'My daughter is scared even to pass by the lane where Payal lives,' the mother interrupted. 'People are still going to say that the two of them must have run off with boys. But the truth is that Payal wanted to get away from her stepmother and Menaka went with her because they were friends.'

We had heard Payal's declaration of love for Menaka, with our own ears. Perhaps at the school too she had given away the real reason for running away with her friend. The act of running away, whether with a male or a female, would certainly tarnish the character of any woman. Menaka's use of the word 'character', in that incomplete way, confirmed our suspicions. But we knew the family's level of denial and imposition of silence would not allow us to probe further or present any alternative rationale.

Menaka hushed her mother and left the room. It was clear that she wanted absolutely no discussion about this subject. She returned with tea, home-made *gujiya* and *gulab jamun*. Yash's wife sat leaning against a steel almirah, sewing hooks onto a new sari blouse we were told she planned to wear the next day, on Diwali. Her leg was aching and she had been given some *ajwain* oil to massage into her limbs. The mother called the autorickshaw driver into the front room and gave him tea and snacks. After he had eaten, we got up to go. Menaka took our address, promising to write.

In February 2002 I received a letter from Menaka. She wrote that she was doing a computer course and preparing for her exams. She also wrote, '... Didi, you are a good friend of mine, that is why I wish to tell you that I do not want to keep any relationship with Payal. Because of her, I have been maligned by the whole world. But that apart, after I left school she said all kinds of things about me, because of which I lost all my friends. I do not want to talk to her any more. I request you to not talk about her to me, from today.'

I think often of Payal and the brave words she had spoken, 'We loved one another and we wanted to live together.' Yet, the story of Menaka and Payal remains imbued with silence till today.

5

Manjula and Meeta

Drops spattered furiously in all directions as Manjula, crouching, beat clothes on a stone beneath the tap at the pumphouse. The swift stream of water seemed as cold as the wintry sky. I stepped back as Meeta, standing next to me, bent to put her clothes down for washing, then jerked away as soapsuds flew into her eyes. She lost her balance, dropping a shirt and a pullover. She blinked, wiped her eyes and turned around, staggering. When she had steadied herself, she ran a hand through her crewcut and smoothed her cuffs in embarrassment. Manjula's hand froze in mid-air, her laughter rising above the gushing water. Then Meeta too burst out laughing and so did I. When our laughter subsided, Manjula went back to raining her fists on the sodden heap of clothes, pausing every now and then to heap it up with the edge of her palm and then press out the soapy water. Looking over her shoulder to continue our conversation, Meeta said, 'We are only friends. It is not what you understand it to be.'

'And what is it you think I have understood?' I asked.

Meeta dug her hands deeper into her trouser pockets and looked towards her friend.

'Bring Amma's clothes also,' Manjula called out. I had a strange feeling that she was trying to distract me.

Meeta left us for a bit and returned with Manjula's mother's clothes, then moved away again. Manjula piled the garments under the tap with her right hand while she scrutinised her left forefinger. Stepping up, I saw that it was swollen out of shape.

'Painful?'

'A little.'

'What happened?'

'We had a fight.'

Manjula is willing to talk, I told myself, while I asked, 'Who?'

'She and I.'

'What about?'

She did not reply. I thought, she is not so willing to talk after all. We both pretended she had not heard the question. I did not repeat it. A few minutes ago our laughter had connected us, but the bond was too fragile to risk further disclosure.

'I have almost finished...would you like to wait in the house?' Manjula asked. 'The water comes only till 10.30 in the morning, and again in the afternoon for a while. We won't be in at that time. The banks were on strike yesterday so we have to go there today, we may not be able to sit with you for very long just now. From the bank we have to report for our duty. We are posted at the orphanage. We can't skip our duty, though it is irregular for all Home Guards, men and women. When there is work, we are called. Things are uncertain; one cannot say how many days in a month we will be working. If duty is regular, we earn about Rs 1,950 per month, it may go up to Rs 2,250. Our names are on a muster roll. The platoon commander—we are in an all-woman company— informs us when we are assigned duty, and we have to pay her something. Sometimes we are assigned to the courts, to shelters or children's homes, or as part of VIP security for inaugurations, etc.... I joined the unit in 1997, but this is the way it has always been. The procedures were put in place a long time ago. We simply follow them.'

She wrung out the last few garments and spread them on the railing of the pump house. Watching her, I once again mentally traversed the circuitous route I had taken to find Manjula and Meeta in the congested lanes of this city. I learnt about the couple from a woman activist who had come with my friend Naghma to a workshop on violence against women. Deliberately avoiding the mention of female friends, I asked her if she knew women who, though not related by blood, lived together. What I had left unsaid she answered fully. 'Yes, I know one couple, though not from my own village. Meeta and Manjula. I see them when I go into town and meet up with my friend Shobha, she works with them as a Home Guard. She introduced them to me.'

Her instant affirmative response surprised me. I had barely tested the waters and here I was being confronted by a wave bigger than I had anticipated. Naghma said haltingly, partly to herself, 'But I know Shobha, she never told us....' Her voice trailed into silence. She looked at me thoughtfully and continued, 'I guess it needs asking, that is what the stories are for and about.'

Naghma's words, 'it needs asking', were almost prophetic. The ease with which the initial information was volunteered about the women did not come my way again. Perhaps I did not ask enough. So, this story though about the couple and their friend Shobha, is as much about the complexities of articulation, of asking, answering and the many silences that fall in between the uttered and the unutterable.

Naghma introduced me to Shobha, who in turn agreed to arrange a meeting with Meeta and Manjula. I met Shobha in Naghma's house—a first-floor two-bedroom flat with all the amenities of a middle-class home. In addition, it was filled with books and seemed a safe, protected space. Naghma left us to talk on our own. I told Shobha about my involvement with the women's movement. When I told her about the stories I was documenting, she remarked thoughtfully, 'It is a good way to live, in fact it is the most befitting way. Women living with women, in a society that robs women of their dignity, desire and free will. I have told Manjula and Meeta about your work about writing the life-stories of women who live with one another. They have agreed to talk. But you will have to do the asking yourself—I mean, about the exact nature of their relationship. I can only take you to meet them.'

'When I joined the unit as a Home Guard, Manjula and Meeta had already been there for two years. They were known as the "miyan-bibi jodi". They always reported for their duty together, Meeta riding a bicycle with Manjula sitting behind on the carrier. People would say, "Here arrives the couple at last!".... The women tease them and there is a bit of gossip, but no one seriously objects to their living arrangement. Everyone sees them as female friends. Once I was assigned night shifts with Manjula, and Meeta came there soon after our duty began, and she was there every single night. You can ask Meeta and she will tell you there is more to the relationship than just being friends. She watches over Manjula like a jealous lover. They always manage to get assigned to duties together, most of the time. They don't report for work if they are given separate shifts. Meeta in fact wants to have a court marriage with Manjula, but Manjula is already married. Even Meeta was once married. So was I. But we have both left our husbands. Manjula hasn't, at least not in the way we have....'

'Unlike Meeta, I have children, two boys, they are with my husband. I have not seen them for five years now. I myself am not like Meeta...you understand what I mean.... My marriage was a disaster. I was married off before my eighteenth year. I scrupulously followed all the prescriptions laid down for a "good wife". I did everything a woman ought to do. But nothing helped, I had to leave. Even my children, I had to leave them, it was the hardest thing in the world, but I had to leave them. My husband beat me severely, whether he was drunk or sober. Any excuse would do to get at me. People in the village intervened, my family intervened, but nothing stopped him. Once a senior police officer intervened and got my husband jailed. It deterred him for a few days. I too was instructed to behave. As soon as he was released, he returned to his ways. My mother is single and poor, and was unwilling to keep me. A woman who did social work in our village helped me. She got in touch with the authorities of the shelter home I am now living in. I came to the city. This is how I escaped my husband.'

Having left her husband, Shobha stood marginalised on many levels, from material comforts to forfeiting her right to motherhood. She had to leave her village and stay in a shelter home for women in an alien city. Except for the days that she found work as a Home Guard, she volunteered her time and services for the home that gave her shelter. Labelled as the 'bad woman', she was caught between what she had been conditioned to believe, and what she was now crafting on her own. Sitting with her that evening, I saw the imprint of that conflict upon her person. She was 28 years old. Her fair face was framed by a halo of black hair tied back tightly into a single plait. There was something about her manner, her whole self, that mocked the austerity of that plait, even as it hung sad and limp. Shobha laughed loudly and frequently. Even the strides she took were far from meek. When she sat, the salwar-kameez and shoes she wore made it simpler for her to cross and uncross her legs or set them far apart. And yet her refusal of tea and a meal with us indicated a certain shyness. Perhaps it was because of the inevitable class difference. Whatever the reason, this trait seemed to be at odds with her boldness. I also noted the quick, assertive little note of pride that crept into her voice when she claimed to belong to the *thakur* caste. Perhaps her upper-caste identity restored a sense of personal dignity in a world which had otherwise diminished her status at all levels.

'I had to support myself. Initially I worked as a domestic help for a family, got food, clothes and shelter in return for washing utensils, sweeping and swabbing. Then I worked in a centre for the disabled. I left there because they wanted me to sign on a pay slip for Rs 1,500 while they would actually pay me Rs 600. I refused. After that I got work in another district, but the commute took four hours coming and going, I walked most of the way and then had to take a boat across the river. Finally I heard about this Home Guard job and managed somehow to get in. Till last year they used to even accept illiterates, but now they insist on a high school certificate. This requirement will make it hard for women. How many women in the villages get a chance to even see a school?'

'After I was recruited I had to undergo three months of training—we learnt to fire rifles, drill, march, salute, run, all of that. But let me tell you, I did not bribe anyone in order to get selected. I had no money. I survived on the Rs 20 we got as a daily allowance. Meeta and Manjula also underwent the same training. Actually, that is where they first met, at the training camp.'

'This is a good thing between two women, I mean a relationship like that between husband and wife. Two women can support each other physically, emotionally, financially. If there were more such relationships, men would not know what to do! In a relationship between women, one will not eat after the other has eaten, or get up early to do chores and go to sleep late finishing chores, or meekly obey the other without question, as it is in man-woman relationships...though Manjula never goes to her village without consulting Meeta. Often they go together. Manjula's visits to the village depend a lot on what Meeta has to say. When Meeta goes to her village, Manjula accompanies her.'

Shobha paused thoughtfully. I asked her if she could be present at my meeting with Manjula and Meeta. She readily agreed. We planned to meet the following morning at Naghma's house and proceed from there. Shobha left, but to our surprise she returned that very evening. Naghma opened the door and called out to me, 'Shobha wants you to meet her male friend.'

'Really!' was all I could say in turn. Without waiting to be asked inside, Shobha introduced her tall, thin friend at the door. He worked as a police constable. They met one another in the course of their work. 'Earlier he had the same general idea that women are responsible when things go wrong. Now at least he listens...' explained Shobha. The man nodded quietly. 'Earlier we used to get into arguments regarding women. But he does help....' When I asked them to come in, she said she was in a hurry. They left soon after. I kept wondering why she had introduced her friend to me. Perhaps she wanted to share a part of her life she couldn't talk about to anyone else? Was she hiding something that was taboo? Was it for both reasons?

The next morning Shobha called to say some urgent work had come up in the shelter home. She would try her best to meet us at Manjula's house, but if she couldn't make it, she would definitely come and meet us at Naghma's house in the evening.

Following Shobha's directions, Naghma and I reached the couple's house after many right and wrong turns. We finally found the landmark, a huge signboard displaying white teeth embedded in pink gums with the resident dentist's name inscribed below. If one turned to the left and then walked another 15 yards, one could reach the house. But we went completely around the block because the lanes were clogged with dozens of meditative cows and buffaloes chewing cud in a stupor with half-shut eyes, occasionally flicking their tails to chase away the flies and the birds perched on their broad backs, amply demonstrating how the locality, Ahir Basti, got its name. The pungent reek of dung filled the air. Dung covered the street in such a thick ochre layer that one could not really tell if the pavement even existed.

Outside the house we met Manjula's mother, who pointed in the direction of the pump house where Manjula and Meeta had taken the clothes for washing. Naghma and I walked there and introduced ourselves, and explained Shobha's absence. After giving me directions back to her own house, Naghma left us.

Now, following Manjula to her dwelling behind the high wall of the double-storey building, I asked myself if I was intruding. I went through the whole process in my head—Shobha had spoken to them about my work, they had agreed to talk to me. But so far I had only received mixed signals. While Meeta clearly called the relationship a friendship, Manjula had revealed an intimacy in that bond, in the manner in which she had held up her finger, sharing the cause of that wound, and then suddenly withdrawing. I was no longer sure how much I could ask, or to what extent I could be frank with them.

As we entered the house, Manjula pointed to a large *takhat* near the door and asked me to sit. She went to the left side of the room and lit the gas stove, putting a small vessel of water to boil. She said, 'I am making tea for you, sit against the wall, be comfortable.' Turning away from the stove, she pulled a *bhagona* from the utensil stand, filled it and set it on the electric heater and went on, 'In a few minutes you will have to put your feet up anyway, I have to bathe my child. In this winter cold, I bathe her inside.'

The space between the *takhat* and the door was the only empty area in the room. It was dark despite the sun streaming through the worn curtain hanging over the door, the one entrance to the house, so Manjula kept the electric bulb on. The pale sunlight and the bulb's yellow radiance mingled discordantly, suffusing the tiny quarters in a surreal manner. The room was no bigger than 12 or 15 square feet. I found out from Manjula that the rent was about Rs 2,400 annually. She added that there were no water or electricity charges: these are the few privileges that the enterprising poor somehow manage.

Manjula had been living here since 1997 with her mother, her seven-year-old daughter Kajal and her aunt's daughter Kiran, who was washing utensils outside. They shared their space with Meeta. When I followed Manjula inside, the only other person in the room was Manjula's 75-year-old widowed mother who was bent, grey and hard of hearing. I greeted her, but she remained absorbed in folding and neatly piling the clothes on a shelf.

Manjula lamented, 'Till recently my mother could hear as well as anyone else. But you see that broken wall outside, it was a bathroom—one of its walls collapsed and a splinter flew into her ear. She escaped injury but her hearing was affected. She is the one who takes care of us, we do not have to take care of her. She is not dependent, she gets a pension because my father used to be in the army. She manages to buy her own medicines and has enough for small expenses. She gives me most of it, keeping a little bit to be able to get treats for the children once in a while. Grandmothers have to indulge their children....'

This explained to some extent why the mother had not responded to my greeting, but the hostility and mistrust emanating from her corner was too strong to ignore. All the while that Manjula was talking, I had a disquieting sense of her mother's resentment.

Manjula explained that they were also supported by their father's brothers in the village, who owned some land and sent them rice or grain regularly. 'At times we bring it ourselves when we go to the village. My mother is quite unusual in her own way. She tells me not to keep any kind of fast for husband, or child, or to appease any god, for as long as she is alive. Between us, it is Meeta who does the fasting. Today is Saturday, so she will eat only once. No tea, nothing.... When my daughter returns from school and the tuition class, my mother is here. When I started working in the city and decided to live away from my husband and in-laws in the village, she came to live with me. Kiran does not live here, she will go back to her own home. I am my mother's only child, just as Kajal is my only child. The other reason why I chose to live in the city is because they have schools here—I send Kajal to a private school. The government schools are useless. We have to pay a lot of money in the private schools, but there is no option. Kajal's school fees cost me Rs 70 per month and they also charge a separate examination fee which varies from Rs 25 to Rs 50. Her tuition fees are another expense.'

Manjula handed me a cup of tea. In between sips, I looked around while she called Kajal and quickly bathed her. The *takhat* on which I sat was pushed against the wall but it took up half the available space. Jutting from the wall above me were four shelves lined with neatly folded clothes. A television sat on a triangular slab in the corner where two walls met. Next to the clothes shelves was another set of shelves adorned with statues of various gods. Prominent among them was Shiva. *Shivling*s of various sizes were placed on shelves near the gas stove. On the walls hung pictures of goddess Saraswati in various poses. Old trunks were piled one on top of the other along the wall facing the *takhat*. Near the ceiling a string tied across the room from wall to wall sagged under the weight of the clothes it bore. A cloth had also been tied below the ceiling to contain its flaking crust and rainwater seepage. Tired bricks peered out as if relieved at finally being exhumed from their damp grave of peeling plaster.

'Stay still,' Manjula admonished Kajal, rubbing oil on her limbs and dressing her with difficulty as she bounced up and down on the *takhat*. Kajal had two fingers and toes missing from her left hand and foot. 'This is Papa!' the child exclaimed, pointing to a double frame of studio photographs set on top of the television. In one frame, against a painted backdrop of trees and a flowing stream, two men sat staring self-consciously at the camera. The other frame showed a younger Manjula, about 18 years old. The camera had caught her without waiting for her to pose or carefully part her lips, for she was standing dazed and unsmiling, her hands stiffly at her sides. She did not resemble the dark, sensuous woman with perfect sparkling teeth who sat in front of me now.

I looked at Manjula closely again. Dressed casually in a nightgown, she had a serious air about her—a demeanour that matched well what the mangalsutra around her neck symbolised—marriage, responsibility, a certain maturity characteristic of married women running their households. But to me the joint presence of the nightgown and the mangalsutra signified the split existence she had to ceaselessly negotiate—the first item was indicative of her life with Meeta, possible only in the relative anonymity of the city, with a paid job, some freedom and autonomy; the second item was indicative of the self she presented in the village, where she lived as the good daughter-in-law of the family she married into, and covered her head with her *saree* in the typical manner of the obedient, subservient wife. The only weapon she had there was her silence, and she used it effectively to counter her powerlessness.

'My husband's real mother passed away, my other mother-in-law asks me why I stay away from my home and husband, she says I should stay in the village. I say nothing in response. I cannot argue with an elder. But I cannot live in the village, here Kajal is going to school, I have my job....' There was no mention of Meeta in her list of reasons for staying in the city, but I respected the deliberate strategy of barricading herself into the tense corner of her unspoken choices.

Meeta pushed the curtain aside with her shoulder and entered the room at this point, carrying a basket of clean utensils. She was the odd one in this traditional context, standing out because of her masculine ways of dressing, speaking and presenting herself. Manjula's marital status and motherhood blunted the sharp edges of those revealing differences, fitting them into a framework of permissible female friendship, and giving the partnership a semblance of 'normalcy' so crucial for social and psychological survival. People tolerated Meeta and Manjula's cohabitation partly because the couple denied they had a sexual relationship, and partly because society itself was resistant to the notion of recognising women as autonomous sexual beings capable of initiating, enjoying and sustaining erotic bonds. Meeta and Manjula were violators, transgressors, conspirators. Meeta was twice as culpable, as she externally typified the one who had taken on a man's role, and lived outside the institution of marriage. Manjula's overall seriousness, bordering on sorrow, was an effort to accommodate this marginality, as well as the ever-present threat of exposure and social phobia. Women are of course permitted sorrow, which often becomes a self-validating virtue and a lifelong habit.

Meeta put the basket on the floor beside the utensil stand. Suddenly Manjula said something which had no connection to her earlier remarks 'My mother gave her jewellery to my chachi for safekeeping, a long time ago. Now she says that if she asks chachi to return the jewellery, she will risk ruining her relationship with the family. So she has given up the idea of getting it back.'

She turned to Meeta. 'Will you stack the vessels?'

I wondered at this sudden disclosure about the jewellery, so abrupt and out of context. I realised that the comment was meant more for Meeta than for me. What was going on? Was I missing something; had my presence been used as a medium to communicate something? Had Meeta made claims to this jewellery? If so, was Manjula afraid to deal with her directly?

Meeta nodded and then flashed a smile in my direction. There was a charming gap between her front two teeth. She unbuttoned her shirt and flung it on the loaded clothesline. Fine blue and green veins spread over the muscles of her brown arms and neck. A broad strip of cloth bound the small breasts beneath her undershirt. When she spoke, it was more a quick mumble than anything else, forcing me to sift the cadences of dialect and her rural accent that contrasted with Manjula's standard urban Hindi. Each time I leaned forward and asked her to repeat a sentence, a wave of shyness swept over her face.

As we talked about general topics, Manjula spread a *saree* across the clothesline and went behind this partition to get dressed for work. It was a signal for me to leave. Manjula's pliable exterior hid the quiet determination with which she conducted herself. It was clear that of the two, Manjula was the one who decided what, when and how much of their private life could be shared with an outsider. Meeta put on her shirt and they both walked me through the dung-caked lanes to the main road. 'We will come and see you tomorrow', they promised. As we stood there among the hay and mud and fly-encrusted cattle, it struck me that just as the layer of dung softened the hard pavement for the animals, the appearance of a non-sexual bond invested Meeta and Manjula's relationship with an essential legitimacy, strength, protection, security, the licence to live together. No one, especially researchers like me, had any right to question their choices or the strategies that allowed these choices to be implemented in whatever manner served the couple best. I also wondered to whom they could go for support for the problems they were now having in their relationship. If silence and secrecy provided them with security, it came with a heavy price.

As we were saying our farewells with the promise of meeting again when we had more time to talk, Kajal came running to us, pleading petulantly with her mother. 'Give me some money, I want to buy....' Meeta put a hand into her pocket and brought out a few coins, giving them to the little girl. I heard the slightest sigh escape Manjula's tightly-pursed lips. The child closed her fist around the coins and pranced away. I watched her small form retreating, aware also of Manjula's cynical smile. 'What are you thinking?' I asked. 'Oh, nothing,' she replied. Meeta had walked on ahead. We followed, and I became aware of the tension between the two women. Unable to articulate it clearly even to myself, I carried home an oppressive sense of unease similar to what I experience when I suddenly forget a name or a word mid-sentence. Perhaps Shobha could throw some more light on the relationship.

That evening when I went to Naghma's house, I was disappointed to find the Shobha was not there. Instead, I found Padmini, an activist friend who knew Shobha from the time she had left her husband. I wondered aloud if it was too late for Shobha to come. Padmini smiled. 'No, it is not too late. It might have been, five years ago. That time Shobha was completely different. It is impossible to give you a picture of the Shobha I knew then—so scared and shattered, when she first came to us with her marital problems. No strength, no confidence to move around the city even in the daytime. Now it is dark, and she has no such fear. She will come. Her work in the shelter goes on and on, there is no time limit....'

'It is hard to believe that,' Naghma said. 'Now, the number of people she knows, the places she ventures into, police stations, courts, hospitals...she is so carefree, she makes friends wherever she goes.'

'But I have seen another side of Shobha,' remarked Padmini. 'She was living in the shelter at that time, and one evening I found her there all alone when I had some work there. She was sobbing, overwhelmed with grief at not having seen, met or talked with her children since she left the village.'

We drank cup after cup of tea. The doorbell rang. Shobha entered, brisk and smiling. 'Long life, we were talking about you,' Padmini greeted her. Shobha apologised for not having accompanied me that morning. Right away she wanted to know if I had asked 'the question'.

I hesitated. Naghma handed Shobha a glass of water and laughed. 'We have not got around to asking how the meeting went, and you come along and the first thing you want to know...!'

'Well! Did you ask?' Shobha repeated eagerly. 'Did you ask at all?' 'No.'

'Why not?'

Confronted, I was suddenly speechless. Pushed thus by Shobha, I had to interrogate my reluctance to ask the couple specific questions about the nature of their relationship. At the pump house Meeta's explicit response was, 'We are only friends.' This brought to the fore an ethical dilemma faced by researchers like me—did we have any right to impose on our subjects if information was not volunteered? Did we have any right to even assume anything about them? Were such assumptions a mode of self-projection rather than a means of empathetically connecting with the other? In the effort to get this critical information, if I was given only silence and ambiguity, then this was the material I would have to work with. If the silence could not be or were not to be broken, I could at least render that silence visible, acknowledge its presence, its power, its contradictions, and its inevitable consequences.

Adding to the problem was my own reading of some tension between the couple. It seemed inappropriate, even indecent, to ask any questions that were based on my notions of their closeness. The very nature of what I wanted to ask about same-sex relationships was taboo, as a social and cultural utterance. It would put the women at psychological risk. What kind of protection was available to them? The women's groups took up and intervened in cases of abuse, battery, rape, and other forms of domestic violence. But sexual relationships between women were not accepted in themselves, nor accepted as valid cases for intervention. As I sat pondering my dilemma, I realised that I was actually quite fortunate to have my three listeners. Naghma was supportive, Padmini was beginning to question mainstream ideology in her activist work, and Shobha was curious and showed a liberal bent. Perhaps her blunt and necessary questions would open up a space of inquiry within all of us, individually and together.

I described the meeting with Meeta and Manjula, the details of their interaction, the tension I had intuited between them. Shobha listened carefully, and said, 'You should talk to Meeta. Manjula is married. Why would she talk? Meeta on the other hand has nothing to lose. She is the one you should approach. It is possible there is some tension between them. But I am not aware of it, I have not observed it.'

'How could I have asked, when they both said, directly and indirectly, that they were just friends?'

Shobha was obviously disappointed. 'Well, it is up to you to do the asking, isn't that why you have undertaken this project, come all this way?'

I had to leave the city the next day, and I did so regretting that I had not taken Shobha's advice and 'asked'. This omission, partly from fear of crossing a forbidden boundary and partly from fear of alienating the couple, within a context of denial and stigma, continued to trouble me for several weeks. During this period I was able to plan a second visit, and resolved to question them more directly about their relationship, if they were willing to talk to me.

It was April, the beginning of summer, when I travelled to the city again. Branches of the neem and pipal trees flaunted shining half-furled new leaves, intoxicatingly green. This time I planned my return with greater flexibility, especially because I saw that Shobha, Manjula and Meeta were compelled to miss the appointments we set up; their lives were governed by the demands of their irregular work and frugal wages.

Naghma and I apprehensively negotiated Ahir Basti's now-familiar dung-filled lanes. I hoped the tension between Manjula and Meeta had eased, and that they would be more communicative. We arrived amidst an upheaval taking place in Manjula's house. Manjula's neighbour, who was also her landlady, addressed as 'Marjeena's mother', her daughter Marjeena and Marjeena's three children under seven years of age were all gathered in that tiny space. Marjeena had finally written out an FIR (first information report) at the police station, against her husband who used to beat her and had recently abandoned her for another woman. The police had caught him with the woman and arrested him. Feeling guilty, Marjeena was on the verge of rushing off to the police to withdraw her complaint and seek his release. Marjeena's mother was seeking Meeta and Manjula's endorsement of the act of filing the FIR. Marjeena's mother had herself survived a lifetime of being battered by her husband. She did not want her daughter to go through the same nightmare, and wanted to protect her grandchildren.

Manjula said to Marjeena, 'Your *devar* had come to the police station when we were there. We saw him. Probably he was worried about his brother. Before the arrest your in-laws did not bother to intervene in your domestic conflicts and never tried to control the violence. Your *devar* intended to bribe the police and get your husband released. But Shobha was there, she spoke for us, we told the police to keep the man locked up.' Meeta added, 'Now don't go there pleading for his release. As it is, the police never take seriously any such complaint filed by a woman. They say it is a normal husband-wife fight that will blow over.'

'No, of course I will not do any such thing, he deserves to be arrested,' Marjeena said vehemently. Her mother retorted, 'How many times have you said this and how many times have you gone back on your word? Why do you need him? Look at Meeta and Manjula, they live on their own, they will help you if need be, and you have me and the children.'

Naghma, who is associated with the local women's group, gave the same advice and offered to help. She added, 'Shobha is involved in tracking these kinds of cases, she is the best person to handle it. We work together, we can follow it up.'

Marjeena and her family took their leave. Unexpectedly, we had learnt that Meeta and Manjula were role models. The fact that two women could live together without a man, was being appreciated and praised. It offered an alternative that had been contextually worked out. No wonder independent women, whether a couple or single, were seen as a threat to the patriarchal establishment. But it was profoundly ironic that though Manjula and Meeta were available as exemplars to people in the locality, their presence and togetherness, the ambivalent references to 'friendship' and 'relationship' found no social space and support.

Meeta asked for Shobha. We told her that Shobha had promised to meet us at their house within the next half-hour. Manjula said, 'It won't be possible to really talk here, all the time neighbours will be coming and going.' Naghma suggested that the couple come to her house, and we would telephone Shobha and ask her to meet us there instead of coming to Ahir Basti.

At her house, Naghma prepared tea and snacks while I phoned Shobha, who said she would only be able to reach there in the evening. I turned my attention to Meeta and Manjula who were still standing, a little awkwardly. Taking them to an inner room, I asked Naghma to bring the tea there. In the smaller room, without the formal chairs, sitting on the floor among cushions and leaning our backs against the wall, Manjula and Meeta seemed more at ease.

Meeta declared outright that the city was a blessing. 'I did not like it at first. But it has its advantages. I can go about freely here. I can wear what I want. No one bothers you here. In the village, no one leaves you alone. Besides, in the village there are no jobs, here I have found work. My village is not too far, I can travel to and fro....'

'I was born right here in this city,' Manjula began. 'When I was growing up my father would say with great pride, "My daughter is not going out to work. She will stay at home." I accepted his decision.' Both Meeta and Manjula belonged to oppressed-caste groups, where unlike in higher castes, it is not considered degrading to family honour if women work. For Manjula's father, his daughter's not working was proof of his mental affiliation with higher-caste values and an economic status higher than the rest of his community. 'Because I was not to work, I was married off to a family settled in our village as soon as I entered my eighteenth year. Immediately I was sent to my in-laws' house. My husband's ailing grandmother was insisting that before she died she wanted to see her grandson's wife. But after that I came home and did not go back to my in-laws for three years. Then I had Kajal. I did not like it in the village, after living and studying in the city. I could not adjust.'

'I have a medical problem. As a child, I once fell down from the terrace. I was leaning forward to break a small branch of the neem tree so that I could cut a few *datun*s to brush my teeth with. Instead, the whole branch broke and I fell along with it. I was hospitalised for a whole month with a head injury. I got several stitches. My father donated his blood to save me. After that fall, I began to get headaches. Even today, there are times when my head throbs unbearably. The doctor has forbidden me to do fine work like embroidering and knitting. When I get a headache I feel my mood change, I get angry and frustrated. I feel I could inflict harm. At such times I don't know what to do.... Recently I had another accident. I was going on the scooter with Meeta's nephew when the vehicle skidded and we were flung off. I cut my eyebrow, but otherwise was not harmed....'

'Do you visit Meeta's family also, and does Meeta also....'

'Certainly, she visits my family, we go together.' Manjula did not wait for me to complete my question.

'Do your families accept your friendship? Is it usual for two women to live together as you do?'

'No, it is unusual, but do not forget, I live with my mother and my child as well. In fact my family is pleased that I live with a woman friend. Even in the village I have a friend I am very close to, my family knows we are friends....'

I thought of Shobha's comment, that Manjula would not disclose anything, she was a married woman. Both Manjula and Meeta had agreed to talk only within the permissible definitions of 'female friendship' allowed to women. Going beyond that line would jeopardise that understanding. Besides, they had just recently resolved some interpersonal tension, I felt sure of it. It seemed unfair to ask them anything provocative or anything at all that would expose the intimate nature of their bond. Meeta too seemed to go by what Manjula was doing—interrupting and intercepting me, she adapted her narrative to thwart my questions.

'We are an accident-prone family,' Manjula continued pensively. 'My father died due to a fall. He had bought a plot of land, fairly big, in one of the better localities. He was paying for it in instalments. It was 200 square yards, he had paid Rs 20,000 and the other twenty was pending. He had grown trees all around the plot and even had a small shrine built under the *pipal* tree which he himself had planted. One day he climbed a ladder to trim some higher branches of the *samul* tree, not realising that the ground was rocky and uneven. The ladder shook under his weight and he fell, the sharp edge of a stone cut his head. A man who at that time we thought was a friend of our family helped us during the crisis, but somehow got my father to sign documents stating that he voluntarily relinquished all rights to the property. A few months after my father was discharged from hospital, we received an eviction notice. We had nowhere to go. Finally in desperation we rented a room. But my father would not accept defeat. For a week he sat on *dharna* outside the district magistrate's office, asking for the legal return of his house. But he was told that the papers had been forwarded to Delhi and there was nothing more the local authorities could do, my father had come too late for any action to be taken. My father never recovered from the injury and the emotional shock. He died within a year of all this. I miss him. He had a soft corner for me. I only had to make a demand and it would be met....'

Listening carefully, I began to realise that Manjula was going to share only those events of her life which were perfectly within the parameters of the safe and normal.

'I miss that house in which I spent my childhood. Going to school with my friends, going down the lane and returning to the house with the vast blue sky above our heads morning and evening, and the earth under our feet. We had only built a small living quarter, most of the plot was used for growing vegetables, some spices, we grew our own turmeric even. The *pipal* tree over the shrine has grown so big, I see it when I pass that way sometimes. Now we have nothing, we live in that one room, you have seen it, we cannot see the sky, no trees, vegetables, fruits or flowers. I like to have these around me, the rose is my favourite flower. Whenever I see one I feel I must touch the petals, especially when they are pink.... I love the monsoons and the spread of green everywhere, no wonder they say that whoever is blinded with *sawan* can see only green on all sides. I love the sound of rain and the smell of wet earth, and the power of thunder and lightning. Because of our circumstances now, we don't have a chance to experience the beauty of nature.'

'You do have a plot of land in the village,' Meeta reminded her. 'Yes, but it is far from here and it is in quite a lonely area, I want to sell it and buy something closer to the city, but where is the money....'

'Selling one's property and being able to buy other property is very different from not having any,' Meeta said. I heard anger in her voice. 'I have only what I earn. I am on my own. I have no assets. I left my husband after one year. I never wanted to marry but women are not given any choice, we just have to marry. Now my husband has re-married but he still bears me a grudge. His father is an *ojha*. He practices sorcery and black magic to control people. Why do you think I shiver with cold even when I am under a quilt, my teeth chattering while others are feeling warm enough to sweat? I have not been keeping well. We went to exorcists, and after they treated me, I am feeling better. My parents are in the village but my father cannot do much now, he is old and ailing. We have a little land and with that we manage somehow. I also support them in a small measure. Here Manjula takes care of most of our expenses....'

She continued, 'I have four sisters, I am the youngest. All the others are married. There is a lot of pressure on me to re-marry. One brother-in-law is especially insistent. But I will never marry again. There are many things I want to learn to do. For instance, to drive a scooter, I know I will do that one day. I taught myself to ride a bicycle, now I cycle to work. Manjula has not learnt it as yet. She sits on the carrier. A number of my friends, like Shobha, think that I do not teach Manjula because I am afraid she may run off and become independent. But if this were true, would I have taught her the other things that I have? Going out of the house on her own, being on her own, talking to people confidently.... When we met in the training camp, she was not as assertive as you see her today. She had lived with her family all her life, was accustomed to being sheltered and obedient, even though they were in the city. She was not given the chance to learn a simple thing like cycling... she has her own ideas and when something gets into her head she does not listen to anyone. She could have learnt cycling on her own too. But she is not interested. That is why we have fights. I'm thankful Manjula likes to cook. And not just ordinary meals but treats like *pakora*s on rainy days. She also likes to make the prescribed things to eat on festivals and after keeping fasts.... I do not like cooking or domestic chores. But I do my share, you have witnessed that.'

'The other thing we fight about is when I go off to do errands, or make the trip to my village. I consult her before leaving. You should see how angry she gets if by chance I am delayed by a day or two. She will not talk to me, I have to do this and that to appease her....'

'This one, she tears her shirt and throws her watch, look, look at this mark here,' Manjula exposed a discoloration on the inside of her upper arm. 'This is where Meeta bit me.'

'We both fight,' Meeta said. 'We are equally matched. But after about 10 minutes of murderous attacking we do make peace.'

'My mother and daughter watch silently. What can they do? They know we always make up, so....' Manjula broke off her sentence. Then she said, 'In our house we can openly shout at each other. There are so many things about city life that bother us, but at least we can share that life. In the village we would not be able to live together, even though we are only friends,' she added quickly. Too quickly, I thought.

Later that evening, when Manjula and Meeta had left, Shobha arrived. Over tea I told her how accurately she had pinpointed my reluctance to ask 'the question'. I would have to change my approach.

'Judging by what you told me, it is clear that this couple is not going to talk,' Shobha remarked.

'Tell me about yourself,' I responded by saying.

'Me?'

'Why did you introduce us to your boyfriend, what point were you trying to make?'

Moving closer to me, Shobha said with her characteristic candour, 'I sincerely wanted you to meet him then. But it is over now. We are not compatible. He keeps saying he wants to see me nicely dressed. I do not see how things like clothes matter in a relationship. I don't possess any of the kinds of clothes he likes me to wear. I wear hand-me-downs, and that is good enough for me. But all this is irrelevant. What I really wanted to tell you when we met the first time, is that I have often been attracted to women but it is only after meeting Meeta, Manjula and now you, that I can actually utter these words. There is a woman in—I cannot reveal where she lives or who she is—this woman has bewitched me. We sleep in one bed when I go over to her place, and there is never any problem fitting in the bed though both of us are stout!... My hand strays over her breasts and thighs and I am always hopeful that she will turn to me, but so far she has not. I do not know what she thinks and feels, what to make of this situation that is neither an acceptance nor a refusal. I have told no one except you, I have not even told her my feelings.'

'Actually, what can I say? If she says no, where will it take us? I prefer that things stay as they are for now, I will have to see what happens. There is no fear of violence from a woman partner. Manjula and Meeta may have tensions, but neither of them is helpless, neither fears abuse from the other. Both of them are capable of defending themselves and making their own decisions. The other advantage is that we can take our pleasure, enjoy the satisfaction of our desires with women, without being considered promiscuous and labelled "bad" by society, as long as we keep it a secret. Such relationships are the most convenient option for single women. But more than all these reasons put together, it is the way I feel around women, more comfortable, without the typical obligations that oppress me when I have to relate to men.'

I thought of Shobha's frankness appreciatively when I travelled home the next day, pondering the complexities and intense pressures of relationships that are not publicly acknowledged, articulated, claimed or accepted. A few months later Naghma wrote to me: 'Manjula came over to my house, for no apparent reason, it seemed. And she made bitter allegations against her friend Meeta. She said Meeta had taken her for granted. She never did any housework, never bought even a small gift for Manjula's daughter. Manjula always took gifts for Meeta's family in the village, but Meeta never reciprocated. She had used Manjula's house and earnings and exploited her. She was now after the piece of land that Manjula had inherited. This was why Manjula had thrown her out of the house. Meeta moved back to the village and was commuting daily to the city for work.'

After a few months, in another letter Naghma wrote that Manjula had visited her again. While acknowledging the initial relief she had felt at the separation from Meeta, she now claimed she was experiencing deep emotional conflict. As she was leaving, she had said to Naghma, 'I want Meeta back, I want to live with her again.'

Naghma left the town for further studies. And I wondered if Manjula and Meeta set up house together again. But I never got to know if they did. Temporary jobs, with temporary addresses and the boundary of silence that surrounded us make little else possible. But that we had managed to transcend all those barriers, even for a short while, was remarkable.

6
Shiela

Our women's group met in Subhash Camp every Sunday in the late afternoon when the residents had finished their daily chores. One Sunday a construction worker called Babulal came to the meeting with his wife Meena. 'People told us about your group so we have come to you, will you help us?' he pleaded.

He leaned forward from his spot in the circle of women. The terrace was dimly lit. The houses were built so close to the others that it seemed that they were reaching across the lanes to embrace each other. Chinks of light fell in the narrow alley dividing the houses. Some houses were tottering and barely staying on their feet: they were made of sticks, mud, clay, cowdung, or draped in plastic; others were made of brick and covered with peeling paint, their doors salvaged from better-off colonies. Above the settlement rose a grey pall of smoke filled with the smell of cooking and wood fires. Somewhere in the enormous chaos called Subhash Camp, in the midst of the hazy outlines of TV antennas, sudden pots of green leaves, clotheslines and sad shreds of discarded objects, dozens of women came to our meetings. Subhash Camp was illegal: non-existent on paper, yet in reality a thriving hub where women cong-regated defiantly to make a difference in their own and others' lives.

A worker from our group asked, 'What is the problem? We can help only if you tell us about it.'

Babulal poured out his woes. 'Shiela Sharma has been living in our house for the past two years. Till now she has only paid us two months' rent. She does not vacate the house, nor does she pay the rent. Each time we ask her to pay up she brings along *goonda*s or the police to intimidate us. Once the police even kept us in the lock-up, imagine, us in the lock up, we who had helped her, this is what we get in return for the good turn we did,' he said, pointing to himself and his wife. 'She came to our neighbourhood with a wedding party. There she struck up a friendship with my daughter Lali. Though she went away soon after, she kept returning. During one such visit she told us that she had been orphaned at an early age, and now the only family she had was a married sister who lives across the river Yamuna. She had no place to go. We felt sorry for her and offered her the option of moving in with us till she found work. Shiela shifted to our house and lived as one of us. For two months we bore her expenses. Then she found a job, so we rented her the second floor. After that, you know the story.'

'What does your daughter say about all this, where is she?'

Babulal's wife made ready to answer but he interrupted her. 'We have sent her to her sister's house. I just do not know what has come over my daughter. She wants to be with Shiela all the time. They were inseparable, eating, sleeping, walking around together. She seems to have discarded us, her own family, like an old piece of furniture.'

Even as he was talking, it became clear to us that at the core of the landlord-tenant conflict lay an emotional struggle, the attraction of two women for one another, perhaps not articulated directly, but visible. It was a violation of the social norm, and as a punishment Lali had been sent away.

I stated that before any mediation, a meeting with Lali would have to be set up to get her side of the story. However, I knew that this would have to be carefully handled, and for the most part by me alone, as in our team we had never till then broached the subject of same-sex relationships. We had to get the perspectives of all parties before we could intervene. I also realised that this case was an opportunity for me to break the difficult silence around sexuality that I experienced with my co-workers. Aloud, I added, 'We will have to meet with Shiela as well.'

However, this was easier said than done. Shiela either left the house early in the morning or returned home late. Some days she did not return home at all. Babulal insisted that we accompany him to the village Shiela claimed she was from, to 'collect evidence' that would support his case.

The village was in Haryana, a good two hours away from Delhi. Being close to the city yet overlooked in the regional development plans, it resembled in many ways a middle child in the family. There was a sense of potential which had occasionally thrust itself forward but ultimately receded. The wide main road broke off into bylanes. The tar had worn off the roads like an old piece of clothing, and was totally eroded in places. The two three-wheelers we had hired for the bumpy, dusty ride swerved dangerously to avoid potholes. Small repair shops of various kinds, bicycle mechanics and welding units lined the way. As we rattled further in, we passed the universal barber to be seen in any village cutting men's hair under a tree, and the standard *paanwala* shop at the corner, with sachets of *paan masala* hanging like a curtain and the eternally smouldering rope on a nail from which men lit their cigarettes. At the end of the lane was a row of unnumbered houses, their cream paint fading. One of these was where Shiela had previously lived.

Our inquiries about Shiela revealed that she had indeed lived there. It seems she had been well liked and well known. Though she did not conform to the traditional image and role of a woman, she enjoyed a surprising degree of freedom and social acceptance in most homes. We got various descriptions of her. She 'was not a bad woman'. She was not linked to any man, so her character was without a blemish until 'it was found out that her job was to sell women'. She had a close relationship with a Muslim woman. They were inseparable. Their friendship was highly visible. When the family of the Muslim woman found out that their daughter was not prepared to marry because of her bond with Shiela, they plotted to have Shiela thrown out of the village. Shiela had to leave, but she returned quietly on the day her friend was to be married, and eloped with her. By making off with 'hamari beti' (our daughter) she had challenged the honour of the entire village. A week later the two were sighted in a nearby village and were forcibly brought back. Shiela was locked up for two days, beaten and stripped to verify that she was indeed a woman. Before being released, her face was blackened and she was paraded around the village with a garland of shoes around her neck. A man who took part in this proudly declared, 'We did not report the incident to the police because our daughter would also have been dragged into the mess. Besides, the whole affair of two women developing such relations would have brought shame upon our village. We settled things amongst ourselves.'

As we listened we could only respond by echoing the last few words of their sentences. The enormity of what had happened to Shiela, the magnitude of her brutalisation, took a long time to sink in. Nothing, nothing had been done to bring justice here. The village men were flaunting their actions as a heroic deed undertaken on their own initiative without the intervention of the law; indeed, probably with the connivance of the police. The episode was sobering for us in another respect as well, in reminding us that we too, as representatives of women's rights, intervened in social and family conflicts and settled them according to our own reckonings and sense of justice. Babulal's triumphant 'I told you' as we departed was like salt on a wound. We rode back all the way without a word.

Three days later we met Lali in our office space. She came with her parents. They sat slightly apart and Lali settled herself into the gap between them. Barely lifting her large brown eyes to greet us, she busied herself in picking up the corner of her *dupatta* and throwing it over her shoulders. She tugged her *kurta* down over her *salwar*, interlocked her fingers and stared quietly in one direction.

We asked her to describe the problem. Without hesitation or shyness she replied at once, 'I love Shiela with all my being. I gave her all of myself. But she has betrayed me.'

Babulal, cringing, quickly turned his face away. But Meena, the mother, looked at her daughter tenderly. Perhaps she understood her? This daughter was transgressing all the social and cultural rules. No traditional daughter makes such statements in the presence of her parents, especially if she is confessing love for another woman.

'How has she betrayed you?'

'She loves someone else. She is with her day and night. I loved her and did all her work—all the cooking, sweeping, sewing, cleaning—I did everything. I cannot even imagine that she has misbehaved with my father.' Suddenly, without a pause, Lali asked, 'Have you met her?'

In the attempt to get more information, I silenced my conscience and lied. 'Yes, we have met her and she says you let her down. You succumbed to your family's pressure. She says that those who betray their love are not friends, but....'

Furious, Lali interrupted me. 'She is the one who has let me down. She used my emotions and my body. While she had a relationship with me she was carrying on with two other girls in our neighbourhood. If you were in my place, would you...' Overwhelmed, she could not continue. Her voice shook with emotion as she wiped tears from her face with her *dupatta*.

The father sat with a pained look on his face, as if tolerating a young child's whim. The mother looked at us as if reaching out for help. Lali wept quietly. At least she had acknowledged the problem directly. Now we were in a better position to uncover the truth. Before they left we pledged to renew our efforts to contact Shiela. At the door we whispered to Babulal that he should not let Lali know that we were yet to meet Shiela.

The next day we reached Babulal's house early in the morning. 'Shiela has just left, she couldn't have gone far,' he exclaimed. We rushed out with him. No one else had seen her. We carefully scrutinised the lanes, the bus stands, the half-open shops, for the 'man of medium height and curly hair, wearing a blue shirt'. But there was no trace of Shiela.

Babulal took us to another locality where Shiela's friend Laxmi lived. 'She may be able to tell us where Shiela can be found.' It was decided that our team would go to Laxmi's house to inquire. Babulal would wait for us at a *paanwala*'s shop—the very shop where we had some months earlier intervened in an altercation between the police and locality youths.

Halfway to Laxmi's house we realised that people were unwilling to disclose where she lived. This seemed strange to us. Generally people are helpful. Finally when we did locate the house we could not tell if Laxmi was living there. We looked around helplessly. Suddenly we saw two women exchange a look as they passed us. It came to me without a doubt that we had reached the right house. We knocked on the door. When it opened we saw two young men and a woman in the room. We walked in and said directly, 'We know Shiela Sharma has come to your house, where is she?'

'I have not seen her for some days now. We had a fight and since then she has stopped coming here. But why do you ask?' said Laxmi.

We introduced ourselves and told her about our work. 'We have come here to warn Shiela. One Babulal has complained to us about her. Our group works with women, and our efforts will be to understand and support her rather than blindly judge her. But we must also tell you that there is strong evidence against her. If you are really her friends, tell us where she is.'

Suspicion hung in the air, but as we sat for a while and chatted to the inhabitants of the house, they relaxed somewhat. Laxmi introduced the two young men, saying one was her husband and the other her brother-in-law. Laxmi and her 'husband' were not married but were living together secretly. His family was from north India and belonged to a *thakur* caste. Laxmi's family was Christian and from the south. If their relationship was made public, the couple would have to face all kinds of humiliation and opposition. All their young friends, male and female, came to the house to offer support. So the locals thought they were running a brothel. That is why people had not been willing to tell us where Laxmi lived. This household was a shelter for outcasts. It was not surprising that Shiela had found her way here. In keeping her whereabouts hidden they were protecting another outcast.

This was also one of those areas of Delhi which had come up unsanctioned, and acquired legitimacy by the sheer physical force of the needs and numbers of the inhabitants. People came into the cities from villages and small towns because of floods, famines, natural disasters, riots, unemployment, and a host of other factors. People looking for work, looking for anonymity, asylum and greater personal freedoms, in the manner of women like Shiela and Laxmi, fugitives who had broken the rules and wanted to cut loose from given identities, the locality took them all in without discrimination and sheltered them all equally, for a price much lower than the price extorted by the current they were swimming against.

Laxmi's house was on the second floor, reached by climbing small, steep stairs to the door. Against the wall of the outer room was a double bed. Beside it, on a cardboard box turned upside down, was a portable television. Madhuri Dixit gyrated on the screen and smiled at us from the calendar on the opposite wall. The inner room was very dark. Laxmi went there to make tea and switched on the overhead light.

Our mutual understanding had strengthened even in that short while. As we drank tea Laxmi's husband confided that Shiela generally hung out at the *paanwala*'s shop. In a bewildered tone he said, 'I do not understand Shiela, why does she have only female friends, a young woman like her? I can assure you she is a good woman. In all the days she has been with us, only once did she turn up with a man. Even here she hangs around Laxmi all the time. After a while I found it strange. I told Laxmi to stay away and to discourage Shiela from coming here.'

We stayed for a while. As we left, we saw Babulal hurrying towards us.

'Come quickly, Shiela is at the *panwala*'s shop,' he said breathlessly.

As the shop came into sight Babulal stopped us and pointed to a young person dressed in a white shirt and green pants. Her hair was very short. 'There she is.' She sat between two policemen in khaki uniforms, her legs slightly apart. She seemed perfectly at ease in the public world of men, one with them, drinking tea. From her posture it was impossible to tell that she was a woman.

Coming up behind her, we slapped her on the back and said casually, 'Here you are, and we have been looking for you everywhere.'

Shiela was taken aback. Before she could respond, the *paanwala* said to us, 'What is it that brings you here now? Last time you had rescued our locality boys from the police, this time what is the problem?'

Still with an arm on Shiela's shoulder, we answered, 'This time the police are sitting right here, they should be able to solve any problem you have.'

'What can we do,' replied one of the policemen, 'we also get beaten up by people sometimes.'

'You would have less to fear if you stopped taking bribes,' we said. One of us pulled Shiela away from the other people sitting at the shop, and said to her, 'You cannot forcefully take possession of someone's house. We have also learnt that you lure women and sell them.'

As soon as we said this, something seemed to change in Shiela's manner. 'I have done no such thing,' she said nervously. 'As regards the charge that I have forcefully occupied someone's house, if you are referring to Babulal's place, let me tell you that I gave the man jewellery worth Rs 20,000 for safekeeping. Now he denies it completely. If you can make him return my jewellery I will vacate the house.'

'We know you are lying,' we said sternly. 'We have been to the village you lived in before moving here, and we have a written statement from the people there that you lured and sold women.'

'My life is in your hands,' Shiela said in a voice full of fear. 'I will do whatever you say.'

Shiela had surrounded herself with *goonda*s, who were eyeing us with hostility. The only way to hold her then and there was to strike fear in her and the men she kept company with. The fact that the shopkeeper recognised us gave us the edge we were looking for.

We said, 'Let's go to your house, we would like to talk to you.'

'My life is an open book, whatever you have to say can be said here. These men know everything about me.'

This put us in a sudden dilemma. How wise would it be to talk of her relationship with Lali in such a public place? As a single woman Shiela had to struggle to survive in a man's world. But the places she haunted did not give her struggles or her choices any validity. As long as we stayed in that spot with her, our manner would have to match the setting. Open communication would be impossible, secrecy and intimidation would have to be our method. The sooner we left the *paanwala*'s shop, the better it would be for all of us. But we took the direct course and asked bluntly, 'Is this only a landlord-tenant conflict or also a story of your love affair? You love Lali and you have a sexual relationship with her. She has told us everything. She feels you have betrayed her and says if you could meet her just once....'

We had touched a raw nerve. 'Come,' she said in a voice heavy with unshed tears, 'let's go to my house, I will tell you everything.'

As we moved off we heard one of the men exclaiming, Strange, how can two women do it?'

On the way Shiela said, 'I had no idea you knew about these relationships between women. You talked so openly about them before the men.' Suddenly everything seemed different. Her initial hostility and unease had turned into a kind of openness.

Back in Laxmi's house we went into the inner room that was also used as a kitchen. Shiela spread a sheet for us to sit on and showed us albums and loose photos of both her and Lali. 'She had named me Ravi. I called her Naina. She has lovely eyes, look at those eyes,' she said, pointing to a picture. 'I met her for the first time at a wedding party. At the ceremony of bidding farewell to the bride, when all the women were standing and weeping, I stole up quietly from behind and held Lali by the waist. She liked that. Then when I had gone away she wrote me a letter. We wrote often. When I began to stay with them and sometimes when I returned late, Babulal would say, "Take care of your pining patient. Do not leave her alone." I even put *sindoor* in the parting of her hair. Her mother was open to our relationship.'

With a sudden change of tone she confided, 'They harass her, do not allow her to see me, let alone talk to me. You do not know this, but the fact is that they beat her up. I gave them my jewellery when they needed money, and now they do not let me see Lali at all. Tell me, is this fair?'

'Babulal denies that you gave him anything. Instead he says that you are staying in his house without paying rent. If you ask for anything back, he may have you beaten up.'

'I do not care. If you say so, I will vacate the house without taking a single paisa. Just let me meet Lali once.'

Our team felt that Shiela should get some money so that she could take a place on rent. While settling the dispute we would also try and arrange for her to meet Lali. But we did not want to initiate the process right away because our team had differing opinions about the case. Some of us felt that Shiela would have paid the rent, otherwise why would Babulal say things like 'Take care of your pining patient' to her, with reference to Lali. He would not have tolerated the relationship unless he stood to benefit from having Shiela as a tenant. Some of us argued that Shiela would not have paid the rent, that promiscuity and its related exploitative modes seemed to be a way of life with her. We needed time to look into the matter in more detail.

While we were making our inquiries and thinking of a way to get the two women to meet, Babulal got his community and other elders around his neighbourhood together, to arbitrate. There it was decided that Babulal would pay Shiela Rs 20,000.

A few days later we went to Babulal's house in the hope of reuniting the lovers. Our entry was preceded by loud barks. To our surprise Lali was in the house, and it was she who held back the white fluffy ball of a puppy as we settled down in a cool dark room with a large television set in the centre. All three daughters and their mother were watching a movie. Though we were served water and later tea, it was clear that we were seen as those who had sided with Shiela, as opposed to them.

Bhavana, Lali's elder sister, said, 'It is a relief to have Lali back with us. In more than one way. When Shiela refused to pay the rent and things came to a head, even at that point Lali supported her and not us. She would tell Shiela all our plans. Now she realises what fools Shiela made of us. I saw through her game before Lali did. She had such control over Lali, she wouldn't even allow her to come down to meet us.' She continued, 'Shiela does not value friendship. I would stake my life for friendship, but she is a betrayer. She told us that she was in the police force. We believed her, the way she was dressed, carrying a pistol, knife and all that. She told us she was an orphan, but soon after she came here everyone appeared, a *jija*, a sister, cousins.'

Lali's mother wanted to know where Shiela lived, and if we were in touch with her. She said, 'We have heard that Shiela lives with another woman now. Those people also have a young daughter. There is no father. It is very much the same situation when Shiela came to us, my husband was away in Dubai. I have two young boys. They should be forewarned about the kind of woman she is.'

'No one is going to believe anything bad about her. She has something about her, a certain inexplicable sweetness that attracts people to her. By simply looking into women's eyes she can make them fall in love with her. She is so supremely confident about herself. We were even prepared to allow Lali to live with Shiela, but she simply proved so untrustworthy.'

Lali said, 'I have torn up all the letters she had written, she used to sign as Ravi.'

Bhavana said, 'Everyone blames us for being so naïve, for so completely and blindly believing her, but shouldn't people also accuse those who deliberately set out to mislead others? She told us her birthday is on 23 April, the same day as Lali's birthday. When Lali's birthday would be celebrated, Shiela would also have all kinds of people drop by. We would end up celebrating her birthday by taking care of her guests, giving her gifts and all. My parents would give her a gift and we two would also give her gifts separately.'

When Bhavana was talking, Lali was pensive, her large eyes looked out with a sadness which almost seemed to say, 'I wish it could have been different.' Bhavana's tone was bitter and scathing. 'I went up and cleaned the room, and there I found all kinds of scraps of papers put away in nooks and corners. She used to do black magic.'

'No one supported us,' Lali's mother said. 'Not a single person. We had to pay the money. But at last all that is behind us. Now both my daughters are engaged to be married to two brothers. We can live in peace now.'

I looked at Lali. But stubbornly she kept her gaze down. We could not meet Lali alone to check if she was happy with the decision. Some months later we learnt that both the sisters had got married. We had several meetings with Shiela, and she began to trust us. After the settlement of the dispute, we continued to meet her off and on. During those meetings she told us something about herself.

'My childhood name was Anuradha, until I changed it. I must have been 10 or 12 years old. I renamed myself Shiela. I liked the sound of it, so simple and straightforward. I told my mother, my name is Shiela, and Shiela it has been since.'

Androgynous, heavily built, Shiela looks taller than her five feet. She is like the *neem* tree—a bitter truth for the society that throws her from place to place because she traverses a path that cuts through sex, gender, caste, class and religion, challenging the received notions of womanhood. Though uprooted several times, she fights back to grow again in places with little water and harsh sun and cold.

'I am the youngest among five sisters and two brothers. My father ran a merchandise shop. He died in 1989 and my mother in 1995. She was paralysed, and my sisters and I took care of her. I could not live with my brothers. They bickered with me all the time. They do not really care about me or my sisters. It's one thing that I do not want to marry. But as my brothers I think it is their responsibility to show concern and ask me what it is I want. Instead, they come to me sometimes and even take from what I earn. I have been independent for years now. In this job at the tourist company my work is to make bookings. But this is a desk job. I like fieldwork better. That way, I can go around and look at women. I am paid Rs 2,200, but this is not enough. I take on extra work. For example, I am going to take these Yellow Pages from door to door. We have to deliver them to different people. It is free of charge for the customers, but we are paid. I have faith. I pray to goddess Kali every day before going to work, and say a small prayer when I come back. I want a job with the police.'

A few days later when we went to meet her, she had disappeared. We walked down many different streets in the same locality, search-ing. Since Shiela is visibly different from the female norm, people remember her. When we described 'a woman with very short hair, wearing pants and shirt', we were told that she had moved. Now she was living in another household on the first floor with a woman called Manju. We met up with her again. When we told her how we had traced her, she said, 'I like to wear pants and shirt. When I was small my mother would make me wear a frock sometimes. But I would insist she dress me in an undershirt and shorts. As far as I can remember, this is the way I have been. But now looking at you, I think a *kurta* with pockets worn over a *salwar* looks great. I will also wear a *kurta-salwar*.'

We had found her sitting in the house alone in her vest and shorts. For the first time we saw her left arm uncovered. It bore the marks of a severe injury from the elbow downwards. After greeting us she walked into the inner room and came back button-ing her full-sleeved shirt. Immediately I thought, 'Can this have been the result of the beating she got from the villagers for running away with "our daughter"?'

I asked, 'Have you been beaten up, ever?'
'No,' Shiela replied with a vehemence that took us all by surprise. 'If you are asking me this because of my arm, I can tell you it was not because I was beaten up. No one would dare to beat me. I was

riding my bike when a *rickshaw* loaded with those iron rods that are used to support ceilings passed me by. One of the rods pierced my arm, ripping it.'

Whatever the cause of the injury, we realised she would never acknowledge the incident of being locked up in the village, or anything that was even remotely connected with it. And we had nothing to verify the story. It would be her word against the villagers.

In a manner that was both teasing and curious, I asked, 'How did you find Manju, and how many women have you been involved with?'

'Don't ask me how many women I have been involved with. I cannot remember the exact number now. There were plenty. But I remember the first time I fell in love. I was in the 8th class, or maybe 9th. I do not know exactly. At that time I did not know about these relationships. But I was attracted to women. And one such woman I was very drawn to taught me all about love between women. When we found one another we would not go to our class but sit under the trees and talk to one another. Then everyone began to notice us, and her parents did not like it. They took her out of the school. I missed her a lot. I intercepted a letter she had written to her parents. I took down the address and went to see her. She was in Haldwani, a hill station. It was cold and dark when I got there. Before this I had not travelled alone for such a long distance. But I pretended as if I knew the place. When I arrived there, the rickshaw-puller taking me along realised I was new to the town. He was surprised at my self-confidence. Finally I did succeed in meeting her. We kept in touch for quite some time following that trip. I even got her eyes treated in the eye hospital.'

'Then there was Shashi. I had passed out of school one year earlier. I used to pick her up from school. I would take her brother's scooter and we would return home after a ride. Once I thought she had seated herself behind me on the scooter, I started off. It was some time before I realised I was talking to myself. There was no one sitting behind. I returned, afraid that she would be angry. She was angry as hell. I bore her punches and tears quietly, it was my fault.'

'In Babulal's house I used to sleep in the middle of the bed. On one side was Bhavana and the other side was Lali. For a brief while

I was actually involved with both of them. Later on Bhavana distanced herself, she was angry and jealous.'

But Manju, she is a different sort of woman, she is the first woman I know who cares for me genuinely. She cares to the extent of actually saving up money for me rather than spending it on herself. She insists on saving, she says that my first priority should be to have my own house, not a scooter. For this is my dream, to have my own vehicle to ride around. I understand that what she says is wise.'

'I got to know Manju when I was involved with Lali. But our relationship began much later. I had started to visit her house. It so happened that there was a wedding in the house and there was not enough room to accommodate all the guests. That night they sent some of their guests to sleep at Manju's house. Since there were not enough beds, Manju and I shared one. We slept together. She did not know that women could have such relationships. Lali knew, she had seen something about it on television and read about it in books. Yes, she was smart, very smart, you know.... When Manju and I were sharing the bed, I reached out to her. At first she turned away. So I too turned away. I am not interested if the other person is not. But then she snuggled up to me. We kissed. Now we are together.'

Getting up, Shiela went to the end of the terrace, peered down and called out, 'Manju...!' A tall, slim girl came upstairs. Shiela said, 'This is Manju, I have told her about you. She is familiar with your names.' She turned to Manju, saying, 'Will you make tea?'

As Manju went into the inner room, Shiela whispered, 'Now, do not ask questions about Lali or any other woman; do not even refer to my relationship with Manju, when she is present.'

Then, switching to a normal pitch, Shiela said, 'I noticed Manju the first time in the market, she was selling vegetables. I thought to myself, "What is she doing in this place where mostly men run the stalls or at best, older women?" I observed her daily, sitting there in the market and conducting her business seriously. She held her own in the midst of all those men. Then I began to buy vegetables and talk to her. We became friends and grew fond of...' Shiela stopped in the middle of her sentence. Manju had come in with cups of tea on a tray. She wore her hair in a long single plait which swung from side to side as she bent down to hand each one of us a cup. She smiled shyly. Shiela looked at her and said, 'I was telling them how you and I met. Manju will confirm that I told her honestly that the marketplace was not a suitable environment for young women like her. But poverty leaves few choices. She has a brother who is the only earning member of her family. He has to take care of his own wife and children in addition to Manju, her sister and their mother. How much do you think a poor man earns? It is a hard life. I also lend them money and I give rent for the room I have taken. Sometimes Manju's mother brings home piecework to stitch. But it is nothing. I will contribute towards Manju's wedding. But on the wedding day itself I will not stay here. I won't be able to take it, seeing her go away with somebody else.'

We asked Manju, 'But why must you marry?'

Shiela said, 'She tells me that I should make friends with her future in-laws. She feels she must marry.'

Manju said, 'It is the right thing to do. Women have to marry. My brother worries because of me. Besides, people talk if daughters of marriageable age are not married off. We will continue to be friends even after I am married. Rather, we will be allowed to remain friends if I marry.'

We said, 'After marriage it will not be possible. You are being allowed to live as friends only because marriage exists as the final alternative. You say no to marriage, and see what will happen.'

Shiela said, 'Manju was engaged to be married last year, everything was finalised, almost. The man was a Home Guard. Family, age, job, everything seemed right about him. I went to see him on Holi. On the way someone threw colour on me and my whole shirt got splashed. When I reached his house he offered me his shirt. I wore it without a thought that it was his shirt and not mine. When I went to return it a few days later he said, "I do not wear clothes worn by others." Then he wanted to meet Manju in secret, through me. When Manju's brother found out the sort of man his sister was being married to, he called off the engagement. I too feel that women should simply stop marrying, only then will men come to their senses.'

We said, 'Many women have actually stopped marrying. There are women here who live with one another, and there are groups who help women who want to live with one another. We ourselves have sheltered such women in our own houses, talked with their families, tried to make their relatives see that there is nothing wrong with women who want to share their life with women.'

Shiela said, 'Yes, now these relationships are also the subject of films. You know the film *Fire*, it showed two women loving one another, it was banned.'

We asked, 'Why do you think it was banned?'

Shiela said, 'Women have to marry. It was only a film, but what a commotion it made.'

We said, 'We organised a protest against the ban, we took out posters, shouted slogans. Later we formed a group called Campaign for Lesbian Rights. We printed pamphlets and distributed them.'

Shiela replied, 'We never got any such pamphlet. You should do that sort of work here in the slums.'

The conversation drifted on to several other subjects. The sun had gone down when we left the couple.

It was the last day of the *navratas* when we next met Shiela. The days of fasting were coming to an end. We knew Shiela too would have fasted. We went to see her. A large framed picture of goddess Kali rested against the wall of the terrace. A faint smell of incense greeted us. Shiela was lying on the floor. Hearing us she raised her forehead, adorned with a *tilak*. A smile of sheer joy spread across her pale, tired face. She looked handsome. The red on her forehead, the *mauli* thread around her wrist contrasting with the blue of the shirtsleeve, the expression of quiet resignation, and at that precise moment, a vulnerability which she otherwise carefully hid. Or was it the tension that we did not sense while we were on the terrace, and that we immediately sensed as soon as we stepped inside the house? Manju was standing near the gas with tears in her eyes. A silence descended. Clearly, it was not the best of times to have come. We avoided each others' eyes.

We asked, 'What is it?'

Shiela replied, 'We had puja today, and I found Rs 100 short from the money I had given Manju....'

Manju said, 'If you have to tell, then you must tell the truth.'

Shiela said, 'At the puja many women came and there was singing and dancing. I asked Manju to dance. She refused. It is not as if she does not dance at all. When she is with me she does shake about. When I was specially asking her to dance in front of others, she could have danced for my sake, but no, she did not dance. And then I asked her, where is the Rs 100, and she answered me back, saying, "Am I a thief?" I replied, "Yes, you are a thief, a thief." That is why she is crying.'

Manju said, 'I am not like other girls, I cannot dance, why should I?'

Shiela said, 'That is the trouble, she is jealous. Anyone who comes to see me, she resents it. I want to live in freedom. If you have to live with me, this is the way I am.'

Manju's eyes were brimming with tears. One of us got up and took Shiela by the shoulders. We chided her affectionately, but in all seriousness, knowing in our hearts that she would remain just the same.

At the end Sheila said to us, only half joking, 'Why don't you begin regular meetings of women here, maybe twice a month, whatever is convenient. We can all meet and talk about such things. You know what I mean. We can drop in…' and then with a twinkle in her eye, 'but make sure there is a bed there…!'

7
Sabo and Razia

Call it Balaghat, or simply 'Sabo's village', the term of reference we got used to, ever since we first heard of it more than a decade ago while organising single women in the resettlement colonies of Delhi. The village was near Kasganj in Uttar Pradesh. After several years of silence Sabo had confided to us about her relationship with Razia, a childhood friend who still lived in Balaghat. We—Sabo, my colleague Sunita and myself—were finally going to the village to meet her.

This confession was a mysteriously alluring chink in Sabo's otherwise dry armour. Earlier, no matter how much she was teased and commented upon for her frequent trips to the village, no matter how these trips clashed with her work in the city and her family responsibilities, she made no comment in response and steadfastly made the important journey. She travelled over frail unpaved roads, hopped from bus to bus and changed vehicle after vehicle, as there was no single mode of transport that reached Balaghat directly. At work and in her interactions she was practical to the extreme, dismissing fancies, affections, attachments and obsessions as being intrinsic to human reality, and a chief component of human action, yet irrelevant. In her brusque, ruthless way she would reduce conflict or problems to the stark material necessities of survival, housing, clothes and food. When we tried to analyse her fixation with her home, first jokingly and then seriously, she deflected us. 'No, that is not true, my last visit was only....' When we confronted her with the actual dates, days and period of time she had been away, she would present all kinds of rationalisations, or say defensively,

'You all will not understand.' After some time we resigned ourselves to her obduracy and learnt to duck our heads in time to avoid her abrasive retorts.

Sabo's emphasis on practical externals was understandable. We had seen her struggle with poverty, and endure the beatings she took from her husband without a word or a single tear. She carefully covered her bruises, and we too looked the other way. Other women who came to our group described the trauma of being battered; when Sabo finally admitted to being a victim of domestic violence, she shared her pain dry-eyed. In all the years we have known Sabo, we have only seen her shed tears twice: after her mother died, when she reminisced about her, and when her brothers in the village sold her mother's house without her knowledge or consent. Proudly, as a self-empowered woman, Sabo would describe how she ran her own household. 'I have set up this shop in my *jhuggi*, and this *jhuggi*, is also of my own making. My husband has not given me a paisa. I am single too, I support myself and my children.' We held late-night meetings in her house, during which we would try to present examples of how customs, attitudes, even law, privileged married women over those who lived outside the institution of marriage. Sabo was stubborn, even resistant; she had learnt that aggression was the best survival strategy and coping mechanism. She used it instinctively and uniformly, regardless of whether the situation warranted it or not. Sometimes aggression worked, and sometimes it did not. Taking women to the public hospitals was part of our work, and as a community leader Sabo often came along. On one such occasion the OPD doctor was a kind, caring woman, a rare situation indeed. In her bid to fully understand the woman's ailment, the doctor asked her to walk. But Sabo, supporting the woman by the waist, refused to let her do so. 'She will fall if you make her stand on her feet!' she argued vociferously. Had the doctor become annoyed and refused to continue with the case, we could have done nothing.

During our discussions on the definition and status of single women, trust deepened within the group and we began to talk about physical intimacy. Most of the single women attending the meetings had relationships with men. Others who felt comfortable enough within the group space shared how on occasion they had been witness to women's relationships with women, in their villages, within households and while working in the fields. Sabo mentioned that her *chacha* and *bua* both had been involved in same-sex relationships. But in our search for the overt and the stated, we overlooked the fact that she was insisting on identifying herself as a single woman and presenting examples of homosexuality. We did not make the connection because we were too caught up in conceptualising single women within the context of marriage, to make room for voices articulating other possibilities. When the Shiv Sena vandalised movie halls and insisted that a ban be imposed on the film *Fire* for its 'lesbian' content, we organised a protest demonstration. During the hectic and rushed work of getting the demonstrators together, Sabo made an impassioned argument in favour of supporting any project that rendered visible the love between women. This culminated in her disclosing her relationship with Razia.

'Why didn't you tell us about this earlier? Why have you been silent for so long?' we asked.

'Where was the space to talk about such things?' she retorted fiercely. 'This was never a topic for conversation, no one made it an issue, how could I bring it up on my own? There was no forum for anyone to talk about women who loved women. Until I came into the single women's group, and till I attended the Tirupati conference on women's rights, I had not heard the word "lesbian".'

'At the conference someone had put up a poster with the word on it, but the poster was torn down. I knew there was a session on this subject but I did not have the guts to go for that meeting. I called myself single only because I felt the one truly intimate and meaningful relationship in my life was with Razia, and not with the man with whom I had been forcibly partnered and who happened to be my husband. I was married off against my wishes, I did not have a choice, how many women have a choice regarding marriage and having children? Razia too was coerced into marriage. What social privileges did I enjoy in my relationship with Razia? Who could we have talked to anyway, there is no women's group in the village.... We had no idea that our friendship represented the possibility of living differently, living with each other. All we knew was that we did not want to leave each other, and that we did not want to marry.'

Sabo's existence in the village began to get difficult and complicated with her husband's presence in her life. Much against her
wishes, she came to Delhi in 1990, unwilling and sad. She soon
learnt to survive in the city and began to earn a living by selling
vegetables. She purchased vegetables in bulk from the main market
and resold smaller quantities at a higher price in the *basti*. During
the next three years she made sure she saved her earnings, insisting
that her husband give her money regularly. In those years she also
gave birth to a son and a daughter. Pregnancies became an excuse
to return to the village for longer periods. Her children were all
born in Balaghat. Now she had four children. 'The wonderful thing
about these births was that Razia and I spent more time together,
without tension. Those years strengthened our relationship.' We
met Sabo in 1992. She told us about her relationship with Razia six
years later. But we were able to make the journey to Balaghat to
meet Razia only in 2001.

I looked at Sabo carefully. She sat quietly staring out of the taxi
window as wheat fields fled past us. I saw the familiar pucker of her
forehead. There was something deeply attractive about her and her
face made one turn around for a second look. Her hair, tied back in
a single plait, flew around her head wildly as the vehicle jolted along
the highway. 'Wait till we turn off the main road,' she warned us,
pushing the loose strands behind her ears. 'We will be badly thrown
around, the roads have not been repaired for years.' She was right.
We were bruised and bone-weary when we reached the village. The
story that follows has been collected over three such visits.

On this first trip, as soon as we began walking towards Sabo's
house various people hailed us like family, inviting us to sit on
their charpais, and offered us tea. Sabo introduced us as colleagues
from Delhi, who had come to the village to meet her friends. Sabo
explained that the large, sprawling village—now developing rapidly
into a small town—had about 1,25,000 homes, one half of which
were Hindu and the other half Muslim. Her mother's house was
in the Hindu section, though the family was Muslim. Most Muslims live near the Idgah. No Hindus live there.

According to Sabo, one particular industry has radically changed
the economy and culture of the village: the preparation of semi-
precious stones. These are cut and polished by machines, then

sorted and fitted by hand in lacquer bangles, noserings, earrings and all kinds of jewellery. They are then sent to other places in India and also exported. Initially local people worked in the trade, but later the occupation attracted migrants as well, who soon took over and became the dominant workforce in the trade. Though more skilled, migrants did not have much bargaining power as they were generally paid lower wages than local workers. The price of property in the village has also dramatically escalated in the meantime. Many villagers earn indirectly through renting out rooms to migrants, who pay Rs 4,000–5,000 per month for sharing that space. This high rent amazed me, as did the prices of essential commodities. *Dal*, potatoes, grains, everything was at least five to seven rupees more expensive per kilo than in Delhi.

Because of the arbitrary growth, competition and sociological diversity, there was sometimes a high level of tension among the people. The migrants were not able to assimilate into the village culture, and the villagers were quick to alienate the outsiders. For the latter, the village was simply a place of work, while the villagers were deeply attached to the land and local traditions, and viewed any change as a threat. Along with this external divide, there also existed an internal divide. Traditionally, there was no attempt at reciprocity or understanding between the Hindu and Muslim sections of the population. We were told, in undertones, that the local politicians exploited the tension and incited people to riot. Indeed, there had been violent communal clashes in the village in the past. But at the time of our visit Balaghat was quite peaceful. We were told that when new mosques were built or old ones repaired, Hindus even donated money for the construction. When *tazia* processions went through the village during Muharram, the Hindu population offered a quintal of sweets. The Muslims too donated towards *jagaran*s and local temples.

As we turned into the lane that led to Razia's house, which like Sabo's house was in the Hindu section, Sabo exclaimed, 'There, that house with the *neem* tree is my *chacha*'s house.' The tree was magnificent. The houses were also big as compared to the *jhuggi*s in Delhi. Most of the houses had windows, which are generally lacking in urban slum construction. We assumed that the sale of Sabo's house would have fetched a good price, but Sabo was not given her share by her brothers. 'That house to the right of the *neem*, that one with the well outside it, that is my mother's house.' Sabo's tone was flat, but we sensed emotions flaring within her. We walked on quietly in step with her, avoiding each other's eyes.

Razia was living in her mother's house, just a few houses from where Sabo used to live. Her husband Faiyazuddin was dead. At the time of our visit, Razia was just under 40 years old. She had three sons and two daughters, between the ages of 5 and 21. When we walked into her house, she stopped stirring the pot over the wood fire and rose, carefully pulling the *kurta* down over her *salwar*. She came forward to greet us. 'Salaam walaykum,' she said with a smile on her face, automatically adjusting her *dupatta* over her shoulders and torso and covering her head. She had broad shoulders and heavy breasts. Her sparkling smile revealed her teeth, small, white and perfect as a row of beads strung closely together, flashing white against her wheatish complexion. She unrolled a mat for us. 'You must eat with us! Why did you bring this big box of *mithai*? Let me finish this bit of cooking and then we can sit together. I was expecting you, but not so soon. Sit, sit! Will you have water?' The lines in her face, the concerned tone, her graceful movements, all seemed to spring from some inner corroborative rhythm as if she had undone all the knots within herself and straightened the threads into a continuous stream. The *chulha*'s dancing blue and yellow flames spread a soothing warmth over us, easing the fatigue of our rough journey. 'We can sit in the courtyard and talk. No one can stare in from outside because of the high walls, they were built like this specially to protect women from prying eyes. I am glad you are here, I will enjoy talking to you. Because of you at least I get to see Sabo, otherwise who knows when she would have come to my house!'

She turned to Sabo. 'How are the kids?' she asked as she removed a log of wood from the fire. The flame went down. 'Let the *dal* simmer a little....'

Sabo responded with a noncommittal murmur, lapsing into relaxed quietude, obviously relieved that Razia was responding to us freely.

Razia looked towards the kitchen entrance. 'This should be *chachi*, I can hear her.' We too turned and saw a figure framed in the doorway. Sabo got up, pulled the woman inside, and embraced her. Introductions followed. Though grey and elderly, *chachi* seemed to have all the vitality of a young woman. 'My neighbour told me you had arrived with some friends, Sabo,' she said, observing us with keen dark eyes. 'So I thought I would see for myself. Razia, you are still cooking, and food is ready at my house. Come, come all of you, come and eat at my house. I have cooked meat. Razia, do your visitors eat meat? No? My younger daugher-in-law has also made *arhar dal, alu-methi, makki ki roti,* Razia, I know you love *makki ki roti,* come and eat, come…' she insisted.

Razia said, 'Chachi, sit for a while, then we will go to your house to eat.'

Chachi sat down, remarking, 'Since Sabo left, it is very desolate. The other two girls who were her friends along with Razia have also gone to their husbands' houses. Only Razia is left, always busy with this and that. I recall those days when they were a real team, they moved around together, went to the fields to get wood, to get vegetables, picked fruit in the orchards, played, day and night with one another, they were always together. They were so bold, even at midnight they used to go one *kos* to see a *nautanki* in the villages around here. They would take me along too. This courtyard was a girls' space, all the men were in Delhi or elsewhere, working, because migrants from outside had grabbed the local jobs at lower wages. Only the old male relatives were at home and they had no control over the youngsters…now, since the team has dispersed, all the courtyards seem small and minds seem narrow.'

Razia joined in. 'Our team also used to wake up early to work. We started at four in the morning. At that time not even the birds are up. We would hear the echoes of only our own footsteps on the road. It used to be so dark and empty. Frightening, really, but we went because we had to earn something. We used to go to a woman's house early in the morning. She owned the machine for glasswork. We could not afford to buy it, so we went to her house to use it. You have to learn the trade. You cannot just start doing it on your own one fine day. We taught each other as we went along.'

'The rods are like pipes, glass pipes you can call them, each about this size.' Razia bent her forefinger over her thumb to indicate the diameter. 'Not large in width. With the machine we would cut the pipes and make the beads. We brought the pipes in bundles the previous day from the shop. It was hard work. The glass pipes had to be melted before they could be cut. As the day advances it gets hotter and hotter till it becomes difficult to work. Since we worked with fire to melt the glass pipes, after some time it would become unbearably hot, that is why we started work so early in the morning. 'In the afternoon we took a break, and then attended to our domestic chores. In the evening we returned again to glasswork. Finally we gave up that work altogether. It was too hard. We got headaches. Most of the year it is so hot, and in doing this work we suffered such heat for nine months. So instead of sweating it out, we switched to setting the cut beads in the molten wax of *thalis*. We got these *thalis* and the beads from the shopkeeper. Our work also involved polishing these stones and setting them in particular designs and shapes. It is a relaxed job compared to other work. We work at home, it is convenient, there is no servitude, nor the obligation to report to any boss. I work with my three children. We earn about Rs 300–350 per day. So many households work in this trade. People have even sold their land and work regularly at this trade. It is less risky than agriculture. Children can also do this work. Labourers, skilled or unskilled, literate or illiterate, can earn up to Rs 1,500 per month. My nephew earns about Rs 2,500. My older son dislikes this work, so he opened a barber's kiosk by the pond, near a busy road. He earns Rs 70–80 per day. This way I know where he is, how he is. If he goes to the city to work, I will be constantly worrying that he has fallen into bad company.'

Chachi said impatiently, 'Let's go, the *makki ki roti* will get cold!'

We went to her house to eat. Chachi fussed over us. 'Shall I get mango pickle? Shall I bring curd?' She sat down next to me. 'I won't eat now, I ate my share in the morning. In a while I'll take the goat for grazing. I will drink its milk fresh.' She couldn't stop herself now that she had a listener. 'Is the food all right, made by this daughter-in-law of mine? I have raised my kids, tell me, is it fair that in my old age I should have to bring up hers? Clean them, feed them? I had beautiful kids, and look at hers, black as catshit! I can't bring myself to pick up such kids, even if I feel some love! All right, I am going....'

She untethered a goat from the corner and followed it out. *Chachi*'s walk and manner befitted her character. Few women have the courage to articulate the hardship of being a mother, and being forced to live by others' likes and dislikes. *Chachi* was one of the rebels. Her candour evoked instant trust.

Shaking her head, Razia remarked, 'There is no respite for the daughter-in-law from *chachi*, nor any respite for chachi from the old man.'

I asked, 'What old man?'

Razia explained, 'He is a *seth*, an ahir by caste. She is his friend, one can put it that way. Her husband used to work in the *seth*'s field at the tubewell. She used to go there also. This was known to everyone, including the husband. One day an electric wire broke and electrocuted a buffalo. The animal fell into a ditch. The *seth* was shrewd. He called the husband from the tubewell, ordering him to pull the suffering animal out. The husband took hold of the horns, where the current was still passing. And both of them died. People said to *chachi*, "File a report of murder with the police."'

'What did chachi do?'

'She did not file the report. She had three daughters to be married off. She loved the *seth*. But at the end of the day, who was she? A poor, oppressed-caste woman, recently widowed. What options did she have? Even if she had filed a report, would she have been heard? These are mere speculations, what would a victory imply? Lastly, what I am saying to you is based on conjecture.... We cannot say for sure what transpired between *chachi* and the *seth*. We know only the fact that *chachi* did not file the report. The *seth* provides for her, he sends her grain and vegetables, her goats graze on his property, his grandchild comes here every day to collect food from the daughter-in-law and take it to *chachi* in the fields. How many men do you know who would extend support in this way, and keep their word? It is rare indeed. Yes, *chachi* is wise, or perhaps she is just lucky. Whatever the case, we know the goodness of her heart. You have met *chachi*, do you think she is bad? No? Well, this is what I mean, she is thought to be bad because she does not do what is expected of a widowed woman, does not conform.'

Razia's non-judgemental attitude towards the incident, her simple acceptance of *chachi* and the entire complex of power dynamics that emerged through the narrative left us with nothing but respect for the bond of friendship between these two women. We learnt how the usual norms of judgement failed in different situations. The entire community kept the secret because the man who was being protected was rich and had power. But Razia kept the secret because she believed in her *chachi*.

After the meal we returned to Razia's house and sat down in the courtyard. I took out my pen and notebook to begin recording her story. As I wrote, her elder son came up behind me and cast his eye over the page but I did not make any effort to cover anything with my hand. I kept writing about his mother. He said nothing, but I sensed his disapproval. I felt intuitively that he had understood his mother's relationship with Sabo. After a moment, he walked away.

Razia said, 'I have lived within these walls most of my life. It is a Hindu locality, but as Muslims we have never had any problems. Our community constantly nagged my parents, "Why are you living among Hindus? You should shift into a Muslim area, among your own people. Be careful." But our neighbours did not discriminate. We freely entered each others' houses and ate with one another. We attended each others' weddings, festivals, births and deaths. The women of the households called each other *didi, chachi, tai, bhabhi,* as if we were actually related through blood or marriage.'

'Mine was a female-centred house, like Sabo's. Our fathers died early and we depended entirely on our mothers and on our team of four or five friends. Today my two brothers are in Delhi, one is a tailor, the other has a government job. I keep things going here with glasswork. Earlier too, it was the male in the house who would go to the city to work. Once they left, no man came here except one old paternal uncle. We used to take his wife out to the bazaar, often *chachi* also came along. Our uncle didn't like it but he couldn't stop us. He was scared of us. We went together for Ramlila, *nautanki, baraat,* those types of events. We liked to go in our group to see brides and grooms in marriage processions in other villages.'

'Our group was well known, no one opposed us in anything. We used to play with the boys and our mothers did not stop us. We tried to beat the boys in *kabaddi, gulli-danda,* and cycle races. If anyone tried to come in our way once we began something, we chased them

off with *lathi*s. Once the brother of one of the girls came from
Delhi. He was an effeminate type. He told us, "If you wrestle with
the boys I will give you ten paisa each." So we wrestled and he
watched. We didn't care!'

'We were quite fearless. Once a *thakur* appropriated a part of our
land and fenced it off. Our brothers were too scared to do anything
but we girls—I can't believe what we did then, we had no fathers
or family males to back us up—we surrounded the thakur in the
road, we had stones in our hands. We said, "If you don't give back
the land, we will strip you naked right here." My brother told him,
"You better agree quickly, or else they will fulfil the threat." We went
to the field, took big mounds of earth, and redrew our original
boundary. The panchayat gathered and summoned us. We, young
Muslim girls, stood there defying Hindu *thakur*s and Muslim elders, and scandalising the older women. The panchayat said, "This
is wrong, these girls are behaving like boys," etc. We said, "We have
claimed our right, that is all. The *thakur* is exploiting the fact that
we have no father to guard our household interests." He said, "They
have taken earth from my field, why?" We replied, 'During the rainy
season mud from our fields washes onto yours, since your fields
are lower. We were recovering our mud, that is all." The panchayat
could not say a word! They dismissed the charge.'

'In our unity we felt secure. When we did glasswork in the
courtyard we stripped down to *kachha-baniyan*, The wall was high,
no man crossed our threshold. Once our Yadav neighbours brought
a beautiful bride for their younger son. But he disliked her. With
great difficulty they got the *phera*s done, but the son refused to
participate in the other rituals. Instead, he climbed up to the terrace
and began flashing a mirror at our group. Two of us slipped away,
went past his mother, greeting her, "*Tai*, Ram Ram!" and we went
after the son with a *lathi*. He raised a commotion, saying, "These
Muslim girls are misbehaving, they are out of control, they are
vagabonds, now they are lifting hands against men." We said, "He
is looking at us improperly, neglecting his new wife—is this appropriate?" The whole village came to know what he was doing. After
that he changed his attitude.'

'Nothing was beyond us. All actions became possible. Once
there was a burial going on and we took spades and joined the men

in the graveyard, since the males of our houses were away in Delhi. We began to dig along with the men of other households. The panchayat was annoyed, and the men begged us to go, saying, "You will dishonour our families, this is not a job for women." We said, "Our men are not here, should they not be represented? We will do our family's share of the work." And we finished the burial with the rest of the men.'

'As children we girls lived, slept, ate, worked together. We had dreams of remaining single, being together. But fate was against it....'

'My mother was never happy, and neither is there much happiness in my life. My father did not live much with my mother. He was 40 when he married her. He earned money by entertaining—people took him to *nautanki*s where he danced. He was very fond of dancing and singing. He had feminine habits and mannerisms and used to refer to himself in the feminine gender. People would call him *chachi, tai, bhabhi*, like a female relative or in-law. His head was always covered with a shawl. He got married under family pressure, very reluctantly. He had a man friend, they used to live like husband and wife. It was common knowledge. After marriage his love for singing and dancing did not lessen in any way. But after his friend went away, my father did not live very long.'

'I resisted marriage till I was 16. Then I was forcibly married. I was determined not to be separated from Sabo. I thought, somehow I will convince my husband that she must live here with us. I will use deceit, use persuasion, whatever the means. But he would not agree to sharing me and sharing our space with her. He lived separately and I met him from time to time. My in-laws owned a lot of farmland, it supported us. Even today I collect money from the harvest once a year....'

'By then Sabo too had been married off. She too tried to persuade her husband that we should live together, and he agreed. So we started living together. She was with me all the time, day and night. He could not tolerate it beyond a point. "Here comes your beloved," he would taunt me in jealousy. To prevent him from becoming our enemy, we included him in our daily activities and negotiations. That way I managed to keep Sabo by my side. Her husband pulled a rickshaw. Sometimes he worked in the fields and orchards, collecting wood or picking seasonal fruit like mango, guava, *mausambi*. And as for us, Sabo and I did glasswork to earn money.'

'When my first child was born, Sabo looked after him. I didn't have to worry about him at all. She cleaned him, fed him, raised him. Our arrangement to live as a threesome continued for 10 years after my marriage.'

Sabo said, 'Then I came to the city, leaving Razia in the village.' Suddenly she smiled. 'Even then we used to meet; I came home every two-three months on the pretext of meeting my mother. I had a dream that our children would marry one another, our families would stay connected, we could continue our relationship.'

Razia added, 'I too had thought in this manner. But Sabo, you did not bring it up. Your daughter is much younger than my older son, so would it have been possible? My other son is younger, your daughter is much older. But even now, if we ask them and they agree, things might work out that way.'

As the shadows fell, the sound of tinkling bells drifted into the courtyard. Razia said, 'The goats and cattle are returning.' We sat quietly, watching the day reach its end. The dusk bound us into a single silent mass. 'Let's go inside, it is getting cold,' Razia said gently. An exhilarating weariness overtook all of us. We turned in for the night.

The next morning, in the orange glow of the sun, with a cup of tea warming my palms, I said to Razia, 'You have told me about your father and his friend, about *chachi* and the *seth*, but not a word about yourself and Sabo, Why?'

Razia twirled one end of her *dupatta* round her forefinger. Her grey hair could be seen through the threadbare fabric, her gaze stayed low. Her smile matched the radiance of the rising sun.

Sabo said, 'You can tell her. Like I said to you, she knows....'

Razia smiled. 'What can I say? You are bringing up such things while people are walking past us, coming and going! We'll go to the *talaab* later, sit by the water and talk without fear of being overheard. No one will disturb us there.'

In the afternoon we took a *charpai* and set it down by the bank of the *talaab* in the peaceful shade of the *pilkun* and *neem* trees. There was just the slightest tremor of breeze and the winter sunlight was warm. Cows, buffaloes and goats surrounded us on all sides. Dirt, faeces, and trash of all kind was accumulating and silting up the far edge of the pond. I was taken aback by its size. It was huge and wide, so deep that many elephants could have drowned in it.

I said, 'Are you not afraid of this deep pond? Anyone can drown....'

'No, not really, there is such a network of water hyacinth that no one can drown, but one might suffocate,' Sabo replied.

The five of us settled on the *charpai*. I said to Razia, 'No one can hear you but the *talaab*, and it will tell no one. So speak out, tell us about your relationship with Sabo.'

Razia looked up and smiled. 'Why do you have to hear such things?'

'You know why. We have come to this distant *talaab* only to listen to you.'

'I didn't know such relationships have a name. Now we hear the word 'les...' what did you say the word was? We grew up together, Sabo and me, as we grew together we came close to one another...so close...what followed was bound to be. We touched each other, feeling and loving, each enjoying the other's touch. We found on our bodies the special places that gave pleasure, and we sought each other in giving and taking that pleasure. What is the meaning of all this in my life, I ask myself? Well, this is love. We love each other. Love has many ways to express itself. I only know what I have experienced.... It is simply so comforting to be with her. We can still talk and share so many things.'

Sabo said, 'Sleeping with men was not enjoyable at all. Nothing like what we enjoyed with each other. But we endured sex with our husbands somehow, and somehow our children were born.'

I said, 'Where did you go, how did you find a place to spend time with each other?'

Razia said, 'In the fields. Also, we slept next to each other. When our bodies touched, we liked it. Sometimes it was not so simple to find the time and space to be together. Even though no one suspected us, we had to be careful. We looked for excuses to be together at night. We would bathe together. Whenever chance came our way we made use of it, but bathing was a regular opportunity.... I would call out, or she would, and ask for the soap, or tell her to come and scrub my back. Our bodies wet and dripping with water—it was the best, loving one another through our wet bodies.'

Sabo said, 'We never liked boys at all, it gave us no pleasure. Even when the boys and girls went after one another, we were drawn only to each other. Right from the start, ever since I can remember.'

I said, 'Do you know of any other such relationships in this village or any nearby?'

Razia said, 'No, but I am sure my elder sister's daughter likes women. In Delhi, when I visited the family, she used to sleep next to me and would touch my breasts.'

I said to Sabo, 'Tell me about your relationship with your husband. Did your parents force you into marriage?'

She replied, 'There was a big age gap between my father and my mother. My father was a widower, my mother was his second wife. So they were almost like father and daughter in a way. My mother was very beautiful. Truly, she is like God for me. I see her in my dreams. I remember everything about her. Thinking of her gives me strength to do my work with integrity. I stayed with her most of my life....'

'I was married off at 14 along with my sister, we were married to two brothers. Our in-laws had many fields and orchards. Much more than our family. But all that meant nothing to me. I could not bear to be away from my mother and from Razia. I would spend a few days at my in-laws, then come home. My children were born in my mother's house. I am 37 today, I have four children and one grandson.'

'Razia has told you how we lived as a threesome with my husband. He was away pulling his rickshaw for days at a time. My whole being told me I did not need either his body or his money. I took up glasswork. Somehow we kept our lives going but there was a lot of tension and jealousy, how could there not be? I realised I had no option but to go away. If I was in the village I could not stay away from Razia; we could not live together; we could not live with our husbands; we had our children to raise and our families to please. I could not live with my in-laws. Though I knew it would be an agonising separation, I decided to move to the city.'

'My husband opposed me. He tried to get the panchayat to force me to stay. But my mother—she was clever, she had it written legally on a document that if I claim to be maltreated in any way, I can leave the village. My husband sold a buffalo to have some money in hand. My in-laws came part of the way, put me on the bus to Delhi. But my husband was very devious. His grandmother lived in a village in a remote and desolate area, about halfway to the city. He told the bus driver—it was in the dead of night—to stop the bus at that village. Somehow I got alerted as he was talking to the driver. I went up to the driver and said, "My life is at stake, if you stop the bus here this man is going to drag me away and finish me off for sure." So the driver did not stop.'

'In this desperate state I arrived in Delhi. I stayed with my sisters. I had a slightly better life. My husband got a job driving a truck, he was never home. I was then pregnant with my fourth child. I started to get sick. After she was born, I had a breakdown. I became deranged. I was put in a psychiatric ward for 20 days. They could not control me. I was as strong as 10 men. I screamed incessantly, broke my cot, beat my head against the walls. The doctor said, "She has mental problems, she needs a brain operation." My brother said, "Let it be, she is in such a bad way, she cannot recover. In any case, we have no money." My sisters looked after me. They carried me into the hospital on their shoulders, put water in my mouth to drink....'

'Very slowly I got better. I began to attend a literacy class, since I had studied for about five years in the village. Gaining the skills of reading and writing gave me some confidence. I was able to find a social service job, working with women. I bought a *jhuggi* and moved into it, not wanting to be a burden on my sisters any longer. By then all my children were with me. Whenever I managed to save money I returned to the village to see my mother and Razia.'

'My eldest daughter is 19. If she wants to have such a relation-ship, I will welcome it. She can stay with me for as long as she wants. She has a close friend who is married, but the girl does not want to stay with her husband. She sleeps in our place. I asked my daughter, "What is your connection with this girl?" My daughter replied, "It is a friendship, what else can I say?" I said, "Will you want to love women in your life?" She only said, after a minute, "I will definitely marry." She and her friend and my other daughter stay at home, do the housework while my sons and I go out to work.

They argue about this and that and then they embrace and make up. Once I came back home to get something I had forgotten and the girls were laughing and crying at the same time, hands all over one another. My daughter ran to me, opening her garments and showing her bruises, saying, "Look how she has beaten me, look!" I said, "This is no fight, you are all having fun and getting pleasure. If you want to attack each other why don't you choose bigger weapons than your breasts!" I know they can't help this kind of affection, nor will I interfere in it, having suffered interference in my own life.'

8
Mary

'I said yes to you earlier, but now I am not sure if my story is worth writing about. The problems I face do not have solutions. All the problems run into each other. It is so complicated. Where should I begin? At this point in my life I have come to the conclusion that I have no choice but to play the part scripted by fate. Even if I accept what you suggest, that I take some steps to change my situation, where will it take me? Will it make any real difference to where I am now?'

I was impressed by Mary's stoic words. We had spent many hours together that day, talking. We had first met in a workshop on feminism and patriarchy. As we spoke, we commented upon how little we knew about one another, and we acknowledged that we knew even less about our own selves. Having talked that day till the sun went down, we met the next day as well, and the day after. Mary's initial reluctance to talk about her life soon disappeared.

'My name is Mary.' We laughed at the awkward and formal opening line. 'Well, it is not my real name, you know my real name but you will have to change it for your story. It is hard to talk about one's own life. Where should I begin? Keep asking me questions.'

'I live in the village of Gomedhpur. I am lucky to have been born there. Hidden under it is a valuable treasure—coal reserves. And on top,' she added, spreading her arms wide, 'we have thick jungles. People go deep down to get the coal, they sell it and earn a livelihood. The factory gives us jobs but the waste it throws out is corroding the rocks and polluting the land. The river from where I fetch water, where I bathe and wash clothes, flows close to my house. In the rainy season the jungles spread out in splendorous green and you can hear the *ku-hu* of the *koya*l on a distant branch, clear and loud. I love my village. My house is surrounded by all kinds of trees. It is so quiet. All my life I have lived here, I grew up here.'

'I have five children. My eldest daughter is married, she has a daughter, and her husband works in a factory. She is happy in her marriage. It is a relief that she is happy. But I still have to feed and clothe the other children. My eldest son is a vagabond. He roams about aimlessly all day. The two younger children, a girl and a boy, are studying in Classes IX and X. The daughter who is older than these two does not want to study. Children do not listen, no matter what you tell them. When my eldest son stopped studying, I sent him away to get trained as a welder, hoping he would pick up a trade and become independent. He returned home within a few days. The money I spent on this effort was wasted. He drinks and gambles. When he is in the house I never have a moment's peace. He drinks and then raises hell, abusing and cursing. He accuses me of having killed his father. What children turn out to be, you can never tell...it is for these children that I wear myself out. When I look at my life now I feel it is repeating itself. All that my son says and does, my husband used to say and do too.'

'At 14 years of age I married the man of my choice. My parents did not forgive me. How could I have predicted that my marriage would turn out to be such a disaster? Within a month of the marriage my husband began to abuse me. He was involved with his own sister-in-law, his brother's wife. At 15 I became the mother of a girl. When I conceived I sent word to my parents, hoping they would forgive me upon receiving the good news. But no, they said that the man who had brought dishonour and shame upon them did not deserve an heir, they wished me dead so that the child would not enter this world. Even as my husband continued to abuse me, within the next four years I gave birth to two more daughters, and then he abused me for not giving him a son. Somehow I endured all the violence, accepting the kicks, slaps and the daily bickering. Then I had two sons, but the beating did not stop. My husband was an alcoholic and a womaniser. He spent whatever he earned on liquor and women. Though he had a job, my children and I would go hungry for two, three days together. For months on end he would not go to work and we would have no food....'

'Watching my children starve was the hardest thing for me to bear. Other people would not give my children anything to eat. How many days can one go on giving? But ever since I started to earn and come into my own, we have not gone hungry. Not for a single day. Though I continue to worry about it all the time.'

'There were many things that weighed upon me when he was alive. Sometimes he would bring his women right into our house. He did not care that his children were present. If the children objected, he would thrash them. The presence of other people did not stop him either, he still brought women home, still thrashed the children. When I was five months pregnant with my younger daughter, he wanted to have sex with me. I refused. He got angry and hit me hard on my left side. Then he urinated on me. I did not utter a word. If I said anything, he would yell, "You talk so much!" When I was silent he would yell, "What is your mouth stuffed with...!" I suffered unimaginable humiliation at his hands. I was even paraded....'

Mary left the sentence unfinished. I did not dare to probe. She locked and unlocked the hands resting in her lap. Her brown eyes were narrowed in pain, and her small frame appeared tense with grief. She had drifted away. She did not hear my next question, and I did not interrupt her again.

'I did not know what to do, I was so miserable. I tried to kill myself twice, I consciously attempted suicide though I was aware that I would be abandoning the children to terrible suffering at their father's hands. I tried to hang myself, I tried to drink rat poison. But I lived. I was beaten so hard, practically each of my limbs broke at one point or the other.' She swallowed hard and pressed her arms and shoulders. Her hands were eloquent in themselves—fingers worn down with relentless labour, creases ploughed deep into the flesh, bones and knuckles bent out of alignment.

'I feel that pain still. My children and I have spent many, many nights at our neighbours' house. My husband went beyond all limits. Once my oldest daughter was going to church with her friend when he yelled at her, "Go and get yourself fucked!" My daughter was so angry, she picked up an axe and hit him on the head. It was God's will that he survived. But nothing could stop this man, he continued to beat us daily.'

'I remember the freezing December night when my children and I huddled under a tree till dawn, without anything to cover us. The next morning I set off with my children to the railway station, thinking we would go for shelter to Mother Teresa's mission. On the way to the station I met my husband's brother-in-law. He kept us in his house for three days. During this time I met a priest from the Christian mission. He used to come to the village where my husband's relatives stayed. I asked him if he could keep my children in an orphanage. I told him how all the relatives were fed up of my husband's behaviour and his abuse of me. Whenever they tried to intervene, he would turn around and accuse them of turning me into a wanton woman. The neighbours were tired of having to rescue me and my children time and time again. The sahibs in the factory had already issued him six letters of warning. My sister-in-law and others endorsed what I told the priest. He consoled me and promised to help out. But nothing happened. Who wanted to take on the responsibility of a helpless woman with five children?'

'I endured the abuse for 20 years. It was a marriage of my choice, who could I complain to? Besides, where was I to go? But in the end I could not take it any more. One day, when my youngest daughter was five years old, I left her and fled from that hell. My husband and other children had gone to the weekly market. I went to the mission sisters, they belonged to the same mission as the priest I had talked to. It was close to my village. They took me in. When my husband returned and did not find me in the house, he waited for a while, thinking I would surely come back. Later my neighbours told me that while he waited he paced up and down with a sword, ready to kill me as soon as he saw me.'

'A week later I had still not returned, and my husband told everyone I had run away with a man. People searched for me everywhere but did not find me. They concluded that I must have died.'

'Meanwhile, the sisters gave me some teaching work. Three months went by peacefully, so peacefully. But a former neighbour came to that village on work, and saw me in the market with the sisters. He reported this to my husband. Soon my husband arrived at the mission, with all my children. He had coached them to say that if I did not return home, they too would not. The sisters asked me if I wanted to go home. I said no, but they persuaded me to forgive my husband, and return home with him. With the eyes of my children on me, I agreed, but laid a condition. I would go to my village for only two days and then I would return to the mission and do the teaching work for 15 days. Then I would go to the village again for two days, and so on. My husband agreed to the condition. He said he thought I had run off with a man but since I was here with the sisters, teaching, my character was untarnished and therefore he had no objection to my returning to the mission. At the insistence of the sisters, he apologised. He made all kinds of promises to me.'

'Having reached a compromise, I had to go. Once we reached home, he reverted to his usual violent self. In the village he called for a meeting of our community. Though we are Christians, we are *adivasi*s and continue to live by some of our *adivasi* practices. We settle our disputes and differences by holding meetings. The elders and respected community members come for these meetings, but very few women attend. And even when they do attend they play no part in the eventual decision-making. Men take the decisions and women have to abide by these. No matter who we are, Christians, *adivasi*s, women do not get the same rights as men. There are certain advantages of being Christian, I can see that. I got a chance to go to a decent school, which ordinarily would not have been possible for me.... I was telling you about that meeting. I was attending such a meeting for the second time in my life. In full view of the gathering, I opened my mouth and defended myself. I don't know from where I got the courage. They said, "What kind of woman are you? How could you have swallowed a single morsel of food, knowing your children were hungry at home?" They implied that I was a bad mother, a bad woman, running away like that.'

'I told them clearly, I did not want to run away. I told them I had borne my husband's atrocities for 20 years. I said, "If this meeting had been called years ago and all of you sitting in judgement on me now had sat with my husband and convinced him to mend his ways, I would not have run away. Who wants to leave their home?" But the elders made me sign a paper saying I would not go back to the sisters. I told them I would not comply. "No matter what punishment you give me, I will not stay here beyond two days," I told them. I gave my husband the dates on which I would return. Exactly two days later I went away, leaving my children. I kept my word—after 15 days I came to the village again. But this time I took one of my friends home with me, as I needed support to be able to enter that space. That day too he was drunk as usual, and the whole night there was bickering in the house.'

'The next day was a Sunday. My children, my friend and I went to the river to bathe. When we returned we found my husband sprawled unconscious in the courtyard. I did not wake him. It was not the first time I had seen him in such a state. He usually got up on his own when he came out of his drunken stupor. I went past him and into the house. But he did not get up again. I mean, that day the man met his end. In this way ended the life of this monster of a man. He died that day.'

'But my difficulties did not end there. My caste, community, relatives, they all shunned me and stopped sitting, talking, eating with me. They slandered my character. They said, "She is free now, there is no one to control her, she will do exactly what she pleases." The kind of things I had to hear—they even said I had poisoned my husband.'

'When my husband died, I had to earn so that my children could eat. I did not know where to begin. I knew of a local women's group because I used to get medicines from them on the days they opened their dispensary. When they gave me work I willingly did it, you know the kind of work we do. Women come to us with the kinds of problems I faced in my own marriage—there were dowry deaths, property disputes, divorce, maintenance, custody rights, rape, abuse, desertion. Our effort is to support women because there is no one to speak for them. Everyone blames women—they are blamed and made into scapegoats for whatever goes wrong.'

'Initially I got Rs 200 for my work, then slowly the pay improved. I also began to get a pension of Rs 1,200. I raised my five children on this money.'

'It was while working in the women's group that I met my friend. As we got to know one another, we became fast friends. We grew so close that we shared everything—laughter and tears, day-to-day lives, everything that happened to us, there was nothing we did not share with each other. We simply had to see each other every day.'

'We had first paired off as a work team, but when the friendship deepened we began to go about together all the time. Our work also changed, as a team we worked better than as individuals. Life changed for me once I came to know my friend. Not that my other friendships came to an end, but the sense of support I got from her.... After so many years, I was laughing, eating, talking, walking freely—everything became enjoyable and meaningful. I had never expected to feel my heart beating that way again, the way it did when she came into my life.'

'No, of course there is no acceptance for relationships between women in any of the belief systems, perhaps more so among Christians. I wonder how much space for such relationships exists even in the thinking of the women's groups. Wherever I am, whatever work I am doing, I always have to very carefully hide my feelings for women. That is a reality I cannot escape, ever—the pressure of the feelings, as well as the pressure to hide them.'

'I told her how my marriage came about. It is a long story, do you want to hear it? When I was 10, my parents sent me to my *chachi*'s house in another village further away from our house, so I could be educated. There I did not get a soap to scrub myself with, nor oil to put in my hair, and for food all I got were leftovers. Even though my father sent the family money for my expenses, I was ill-treated. I went to a mission school there—walking through the jungle and then crossing the river, I walked eight kilometers to reach the school. Before school there were the household chores to be done—milking the cow, shaping the cowdung into cakes for fuel, cleaning, sifting the grain, washing utensils, fetching water and firewood—I had to do all this work, except the cooking. When I was in Class X, I fell in love with a boy. We did not get the chance to meet often, so we wrote letters to each other. One of the sisters in the school found my letters and immediately called my father. He was so angry when he arrived, without a word he just took hold of a log of wood and beat me before taking me home. Later I met that boy and told him everything. He asked me to come to his house. I ran away from my parents' house to his place. The people of our community confronted my father, and called a meeting where it was decreed I should marry the boy. Without any further ado, immediately after the meeting I was married off, against the wishes of my parents.'

'There is a great difference between relationships of men with women and those of women with women. With men and marriages, everything is in the hands of the man. But with women, we can talk. Before we started a relationship, my friend and I talked about everything. There is a mutuality amongst women that cannot exist between men and women. I am not in a relationship with that friend now, but I believe we will be friends again. There is no bitterness. And the memory of our love—it is as precious as gold. We were friends, yes, that is the difference, not master and slave.'

'My friend too is married—husband and wife are happy together. He works in the factory. They have two daughters and two sons. All the children are studying. She is married into a well-to-do family. Her parents live in Tarapur. Their house is in the middle of the forest. Her mother, father, brothers and sisters live there. She lives in Seemul. Unlike me, she has a *pukka* house. It has eight rooms and a verandah that runs round the whole house. I have just these two rooms and a verandah. These cracks on the walls—I look at them and wonder where I will get the money to repair them. There is no bathroom in my house. I have to fetch water from the river. My friend has a lot of land, she has a well too. The harvests from her fields provide enough grain to last for years.'

'We both love to dress up. Since I am single, if I dress up here the people from my community, and outsiders too, will say, "She is growing younger, the way she dresses up, look at her." So all my enjoyment in dressing up has to be suppressed. I do not dress up here, only when I go to some other place. I like to wear *salwar-kameez*, it is so freeing. I like dark maroon *bindi*s, and my favourite colour is light pink.'

'I think we made a good couple. We had the same expectations from each other. Even though we lived in separate houses, we lived like a family. We also took care of each other's children. Sometimes she would come over to stay with me, and sometimes I would go over to her place. We live about an hour-and-a-half apart. Once when she had a fight with her husband, she came over to my house and stayed with me for a month. Her husband came to fetch her back. But I did not let her go. I asked him to apologise, and took a written statement from him to that effect and made him sign it. He agreed to all the conditions I laid down, even that he was not going to be aggressive with his wife. He is scared of me. He calls me "didi". I think he is suspicious about us, but he does not openly confront us or ask us. He does not object when I go and live with them. Yes, he is scared of me, but the fact is, he would rather not know....'

'We stood up for one another. Inseparable, loving and trusting though we were, someone created a misunderstanding between us, and we grew apart for some time. Our work team did not like us being together, they resented our closeness. They would say, "If women have such relationships with one another, there will be no children, no families, how will the world continue?" My friend and I both feel that people support only male-female relationships. These have a sanction. The highest legitimacy is given to marriages—those marriages that are decided by the family. When we had this misunderstanding, we finally talked with one another and cleared it up. We got together again. Our friendship became stronger. We became such friends—how can I describe such friendship? We did not even have to talk to one another, we looked into one another's eyes, and understood. It is something very deep, as if we always knew one another. It feels as if I have come home at last, as if I have found myself at last. All I can say is, we were crazy about one another.'

'Our friendship kept becoming an issue in our work group. Many meetings were held on account of us, in the office. Another time, we were both called prostitutes. Colleagues wanted to see us separated. There were rumours about us, and allegations were made against us. We found out that these were being spread by our team members. What hurts is that there is no space for women like us even in a group like ours. It is here that we dream of reforming society and changing the world...and it is in this very place that we face opposition. It saddens me because the years with this group, where we found each other, have been the happiest in her life, as well as mine, up till now....'

'Because we were constantly facing opposition, we tried to think of ways to stop people from interfering with us and ways to stop our team from going against us. My friend is amazing—she suggested that I become her husband's co-wife. Her husband too was willing.'

'I asked for some time to think about it. Four years passed. Somehow I could not come to terms with the proposal. I have been through many training workshops conducted by women's groups. These spaces give me a chance to explore and think deeply about myself. I understand a lot of things much better than before about the way patriarchy controls women and our autonomy and desires. Right at the beginning when I became close to my friend, I immediately recognised what I felt for her. After a long time I approached her, asked her if we could become friends. She too asked for time to think over it. I gave her the time and space. I am hopeful even now, even when I am no longer in a relationship with her that we will come together again. It is something I cannot explain, how I feel around her. Touching each other, giving and taking pleasure, is all a part of that love and friendship we have for one another. I feel blessed by God for having had such a friend. What will happen to us in the future—that is all in God's hands. We have not been able to take a decision to separate completely, so far. I do not know how we will break this deadlock.'

'When I joined the women's group I felt my life change. My team understood what I had been through in marriage, but in my relationship with my friend, no one supported us. When we were having problems there was no one to intervene. Look at the way people intervened to get me married to my husband even against my parents' wishes. Again, during the marriage when I left my husband and took shelter with the sisters, people intervened and sent me back to him. When he died, people boycotted me. But there is no one in our group to whom I can turn when I need to talk to someone about my friend. The team members are hostile, and even my friend may not like it.'

'I am not at peace, perhaps she too is not at peace. Right now our group seems to be coming apart from within. I wonder if we can build it up again. Competing with one another in our work, rivalries, petty differences, serious complaints.... Sometimes I want to leave it all, but my heart is still in it. I cannot leave it. Despite the fights and everything else, there is something here, and leaving it would mean I have lost courage. There are times when I think it is useless to live. After all, who am I—merely a human body, "dust art thou and unto dust thou shalt return".... I do not have a body made of iron, nor a mind like a machine. After all, the body and mind can only take that much, and no more.'

'Our group no longer has funds. Soon I will be without a monthly salary. That means I will be in a deep financial crisis. What am I to do about these children? What to give them to eat? They are growing, their expenses are increasing. I too have expenses, and I have developed ulcers. I go to a private doctor. Who knows if I will be cured. I desperately need money. I am the one who is working and supporting my children, and they behave so badly, what will happen when I am worn out and old and no longer able to work and earn my living?'

'Earlier, I had the full support of my friend. Now I am where I was earlier. I have not been able to make a new friend. I am alone now. But she has found another friend now. That woman is from among our group. I have tried so many times not to be jealous of them, but I see them and anger wells up inside me. What am I to do? I try to reason like this—that this very group that denied our love and refused us understanding is the place where she has found her new friend. Maybe the group has developed a better idea of women's relationships with one another. So I try not to mind. But it gives me little consolation.'

'I tell myself that love is like a flowing river. If I try to prevent or control it, how am I different from others who did the same with me? So I am caught between these extreme emotions of jealousy and objectivity. But it is hard.... Then I tell myself, whatever will happen, will happen. I will make some arrangements for myself, I do not want to depend on any one. Right now I have full confidence in my ability to work and earn. So long as I have strength in my body, I will work...I try to stay happy. I keep busy in my work.'

'I have not been able to talk about all this to anyone else. Talking helps. I feel more confident. You are right—I need to take better care of myself. Instead of merely accepting the situation like a given, I need to do something for myself...I will think of ways to raise money, and also be on the lookout for more options.'

9
Juhi

She settled down on the floor across from me, her face solemn. I protested against her doing so because she had insisted I sit on the mattress. 'No, this is better, I like the cool feel of the bare floor...wait, wait,' she said, and stood upright suddenly in an agile manner. 'If we have to talk to one another honestly, I want to sit facing you.' She bent and picked up a small square mat and arranged herself on it. 'Will this do?'

She was five feet tall, lean, her movements supple and swift. With one action she had accomplished what was mutually acceptable. She tilted her head slightly, rested it on her palm, and scrutinised me.

'You are so quick,' I remarked.

'I used to be a sportswoman. I played *kabbadi*. I represented my school in *kabbadi*, we were sent to Calcutta to play matches. I also ran in the 400 metre and 1,500 metre races. I was good at long jump and shot put. I am not half as active as I used to be earlier. Life changed when I got married. The trouble is, we know what marriage can turn out to be, everything around us tells us so, and still we go for it.'

'I was born in a small village in 1962, the year the Chinese attacked India, in the middle of a blackout. Probably that is why I am such a fighter, why I try to resist....'

'In 1982 I got married. You can count how old I was when I got married—quite young, in the first year of college. I would have been about 20, right?' She counted on her fingers in the local dialect. 'Yes, that is right. I was 20 years old. It was a marriage of my choice. We are Christians. The man I married was from a Dalit community. He lived right next to our house. Anticipating trouble, we went to the court and put in our papers for marriage quietly. For a month the court displayed the notice on a board in case anyone had objections. If there were no objections, the marriage could go ahead. I got married in my parents' house. What a *hungama* our marriage created.... I do not want to even remember it or talk about it. It is over and done with. I had to accept the Hindu religion, and this ultimately worked in my favour when I wanted to divorce him.'

'I got married during the time when the demand for Dalit reservation was at its peak, marches, protests, meetings and demonstrations. There were riots in our state over this issue, you know?' She puckered her eyebrows in recollection. 'And this man I had married was active in the Dalit movement. He was in a Dalit organisation. Whatever happened with regard to our personal relationship is one thing, but I acknowledge that I learnt a lot from him, about Ambedkar as a leader and what he represents for Dalits, I learnt about about class oppression, about caste atrocities....'

'I left my husband after 12 years. But it is barely a year since I have been able to put all that behind me. I nearly went crazy, getting hysterical, I had terrible nightmares. My whereabouts were a closely guarded secret by the activist friends who supported my separation because my husband would come home drunk and create a lot of trouble.' Juhi touched her face with the tips of her fingers. 'I was not dark like this. I was reasonably fair. It is only now that I am getting my colour back. I could have left the man earlier, but where could I have gone with three children, and that too all of them girls. My husband wanted a son. He used to beat the girls along with me.' She pointed to a framed photo on the wall, then rose and took it down, holding the frame close. 'Here they are, all of them. You can have a look.'

The sisters stood with their arms flung over one another, bending forward as if in the throes of uncontrollable laughter, their faces young and shining with innocence and hope—a hope that can only come with youth.

'All three of them have large eyes like their father. They look alike but they are different. I got this photo taken when my eldest one,

Anjali, was leaving for Mumbai. The one standing on the right, she is Anjali. She is studying and she works as well—as a trainer in some marketing firm. She lives with other girls in a rented room. She sings so well. She has received vocal training at the Gandharva Vidyalaya. She cleared her first year and now has to undergo two more years of training. She has a deep, husky voice and people say she sounds like the Pakistani singer Reshma. I taught her the first song she ever sang—it was about *mehendi*. She also sings the women's movement songs. She is more a friend than a daughter to me. She saw at close quarters what I was going through and supported my divorce. She used to defend me when my husband beat me up. When I left him she was only in Class V. She went to Mumbai four months ago, I miss her....'

Juhi's voice faltered and tears welled up in her eyes. Swallowing hard, she paused for a while. 'I named my daughters in such a way that the last syllables of one become the first letters of the next one's name. After Anjali comes Leena, the middle child. She was in Class III when I left my husband. She is an introvert. I was not able to look after her the way I wanted to when she was a baby because when she was just four months old I conceived my third daughter. The third child was born premature, at seven months. She was so frail I thought she would not survive, but she did, somehow....'

'Her name is Nalini, her pet name is Chotu. She is now in Class XI. She stays with the sister of Kailash, the man I now live with.'

'I had a Copper-T inserted after the second daughter but some-how Chotu was conceived. She had a twin brother who died, but she survived. When she had just started to walk, on her pudgy little feet, her arms stretched out to explore the world unsteadily, she fell through the railing. It happened right before my eyes, before I could move. I was alone. I did not know what to do. I remember that sinking feeling, the desperate fear that I would lose this child. At that time my husband used to sell readymade clothes on the pavement. He came home for some reason, I can't recall what. We rushed to the hospital with another activist. The doctor gave Chotu some ice cream and she vomited. The X-rays showed nothing. The doctor could not believe she had fallen from the third floor....'

'My Chotu has escaped death many times. She is special, I tell you, so special.... She wears only boys' clothes. The only time she wears a skirt is when she goes to school in her school uniform. People often think that she is a boy. She looks like a boy, you will meet her when she comes from school, around 1.30...then you will understand what I mean.'

'It is a blessing to have daughters, I did not want sons, I know what men are all about. All my daughters are lesbians. Oh yes! I know the word "lesbian". So do my daughters. When they were young I used to read the Shakespeare play "As You Like It" to them. In that play two women love each other. Have you read it? If Chotu is asked directly, she says she is a lesbian because she loves women. I fully support my daughters' choice. It is better and far wiser to be this way than to marry men.'

'My girls are young now, they have a right to explore who they are or choose what they want to be. As a mother I want to enable their development, growth or understanding—whatever you may call it. Should any one of them decide to live with a man or marry one, I will support their choice. I am the last one to go against their wishes. But frankly, I do not like the prospect much. I asked myself what I would do should this situation arise. After all, I too was married to a man once, and now I am living with one. But I am not married to Kailash. People gossiped about us before I left my husband, and later when I began living with Kailash they urged me to marry him. I was getting a bad name, so were the friends who supported my separation and divorce. Kailash's sister said this situation would not be good for me as a woman. I would be slandered and I would feel insecure. But for me, one marriage was enough. Though I am lucky: Kailash is not like most men. You saw him this morning, he was helping me in the kitchen...he is good. This is his routine before he he goes to the office, he does work around the house. He knows about my daughters' sexual preference; maybe he finds it difficult to accept, but at least he is open to the idea that one can have different kinds of relationships.'

'He has been a father to my daughters. They call him Kaka. When I was married, Kailash used to come to our house. My husband and he were together in the movement for Dalit reservations. Though he himself is an upper-caste man, as a matter of fact, he is supposed to belong to the highest caste. But he is progressive. He saw how my husband used to get drunk and beat me up. Kailash would try to intervene but the next day my husband would be even worse. At that time, Kailash gave me an essay by Saratchandra to read, it was called "Naari Ka Moolya" (The Value of a Woman). It transformed my life. When I read it I thought it was a mirror of my convictions. It was so well-written. All women can relate to it. I have it with me among all those books you saw in the room behind the kitchen. Books, these mattresses and a few utensils—these are the only things we own.'

'The house we are living in belongs to someone else—a single woman—an exceptional person. She put up such a valiant struggle in this life and she too has only daughters.' Juhi raised two fingers to indicate the number. 'Both are settled in the US. Right now she too is in America. One of her daughters is seriously sick. She herself is old. She wants to live in the US now so she wants to sell this house. Most of the things you see in the house are hers—this sideboard, the cupboards in the room, the entire luggage up in the attic, all belong to her. We are only caretakers till the house is sold. But we do not have the money to buy it. Though I wish I could buy it. We have to move around so much. Living in a decent locality like this one will be so good. Though it is crowded, up here the noise is filtered out, and the market is so close by, even Chotu's school. But this property is in a prime area and we do not have the amount required to buy such a house. The woman wants about Rs 5 lakh....'

'The money we earn is decent enough, it takes care of our food, clothing, some medical expenses, school fees, and so on. I do not work. Like I said, the children were so young when I left my husband. I had to take care of them and I was not in a fit condition myself. I help Kailash with his translation work—that keeps me busy. I do not waste time in doing housework, the same old arduous tasks over and over. In my spare time I make cotton quilts. I put all the old discarded material inside a new cover which I neatly embroider with fine small stitches. It looks good. I get up early in the morning because Chotu goes for tuitions. This year she will take her Class XI exams, so she needs tuitions. Then I lie down for some time and begin the day a little later with a cup of tea and the newspaper. Cooking, washing—I do all that, it is not a bother. I use shortcut methods; otherwise housework is an unending business. One has to put an end to it oneself.'

'I spent my childhood in a village not far from this city. I lived and studied till Class VIII there. I grew up in my grandmother's house in a joint family. My mother was a teacher. She had to go a long way off to her job, and she had a difficult time taking care of me. I am the eldest in the family. I have two more brothers. You know why I wanted daughters. My mother has three sisters. When they meet up they all have such fun. They really get along. One *masi* did not marry. She is the one I am really fond of. She looked after me. Even now when I am in a spot of trouble, or if I am sick or worried, I call her and tell her my problems. When I go there I can never return on the day I have planned to come back. I do not know what happens to me. When I went and married against everyone's wishes, my aunt was the one who said, "There is no point severing ties with her." My mother, my aunt, my grandparents—we would meet up quietly without letting my father know, as he was dead against my marriage. He had broken off all ties with me. It was only when he got a paralytic stroke that I was called home and then I saw him. Soon afterwards he died.'

'The only place I really like on this earth is my village. Thatched huts made of hay, mud, wood—the fields and the trees and the silence of the night fragrant with the smell of nature. Almost everyone has a cow or a buffalo there. Our house had a pond on the western side. There are two huge trees, one tamarind and one peepal. As children it was around them that we made our game; we called it "aamli aur peepali", after the trees. This game is something like hide-and-seek. We climbed up a tree and whoever's turn it was to catch would ask us from below which tree we had climbed. When we shouted the name of the tree, that person would try to reach us. We would slide or jump, or tease him/her by jumping from branch to branch. That was such fun. Boys and girls would play the game together.'

'We also studied together. There were no separate schools. In a way it is a better practice. Not like the convent schools or other city schools where the children are separated. We grew up knowing about the other sex, so there was no particular interest or curiosity.

There are many things books cannot teach—this is one of them, isn't it? There are some good things about the convent schools. They teach well, and to learn in the English medium is good in the long run. Otherwise, not knowing English is another dividing factor; anyone who knows English is considered superior to someone who does not know the language. One can also communicate with different kinds of people with English. After all English has become the common language. All the years that my children were studying, I tried to get them admitted in a convent school. Finally, only Chotu has managed to get in. You know how she got admission? On the basis of reservation for Dalits, not as a Christian, although it is a convent school....'

Juhi stopped talking and got up to open the door. 'This is Chotu.' A shy, dark girl in a skirt and blouse walked into the room. She had short hair and a dense mat of curly lashes shading her eyes. A school satchel was already partially sliding off her shoulder. Shrugging it onto the sideboard, she looked questioningly at her mother. She had large eyes, just as Juhi had mentioned. Juhi introduced me. 'Auntie is here to write about my life and my relationships with women. You know what? I think every woman is a lesbian at heart. What does it mean when women say, "This is my best friend?" Indirectly they are expressing their love for women. This is my personal opinion. Women love one another....'

Leaving her declaration unfinished, she changed her tone and addressed me warmly. 'Don't worry.' She had sensed my discomfort. 'I told you, my children know how I feel. We talk about it all the time. My daughters and I—we share everything with each other. Their friends tell me how lucky my kids are that they can talk to me easily and share the stories of their heartaches and their happiness.... We will talk more. Let us eat first.'

Meanwhile, Chotu had slipped out of her skirt and stretched out on the floor in her shorts and blouse. Juhi went into the kitchen and called to Chotu to set some plates out. I followed Juhi into the kitchen. It was neat and tidy like the rest of the house, and similarly sparse. Unlike most households, this one did not have a refrigerator. I offered to help with the meal. Juhi refused firmly. 'It will not take a minute.' Soon a simple meal was laid out where we were sitting. Juhi flitted with lightning speed between the kitchen and the drawing-dining room, carrying hot *chapati*s to us.

'Chotu will sleep for a while after we eat, right?' She looked towards her. 'If you have finished, go to sleep.' Looking at me, she explained, 'She gets up so early.'

'I will go in a little while,' Chotu said.

Juhi returned to the kitchen and came back with her plate. I asked Chotu about her school and the subjects she had taken. 'Science, I have taken science,' she said in a tone which implied that she would not have chosen anything else. 'I want to become a doctor. I know it is a tough field with a lot of competition but I want to try.'

'This is the first time that she is taking tuitions; throughout she has studied on her own and has done quite well. But she has to do very well to get admission and to be able to do the course of her choice. Why don't you take a quick nap, Chotu?' Juhi added.

Chotu reluctantly got up and went into the other room. We sat up to talk, but when the rain-scented monsoon breeze began blowing in through the windows of the fourth-floor flat, we too began to feel drowsy. Later Juhi got busy with her evening chores and further dialogue was not possible.

We met a few times again. On one holiday Chotu also joined us. 'Tell her,' Juhi laughed, 'tell her how that day they would not let you inside the school....'

Chotu plunged into the story. 'There was some function in the school and we had all dressed up. The girls wore *saree*s and I wore pants and shirt. The guard at the gate would not allow me in, until I told him I was Chotu. That day there was quite a commotion in the school too, everyone thought that a boy had walked into the school compound. There are some girls in my class who are always looking to grab the seat next to mine. They like to sit next to me. You can easily tell what is going on. I have a friend with whom I like to sit. She is good at her studies and good at heart. I am fond of her, we get along well. My mother has met her. But there are times this boy-girl mix-up has got me into trouble. Recently there was an inter-school debate and some of us from our school went to another school. There I saw a pretty girl. I smiled at her but she did not return the smile. Instead, she stared back at me. When I smiled again she walked up to me and slapped me. The others around us told her I was a girl, and she apologised. But I did not return her smile. She had slapped me.'

'There are some tenants on the top floor,' Juhi added. 'Three working women. They are in the police or the army. In the evenings all of them come out and look at my girls. I can tell they are lesbian women. We—mother and daughters—have a code word for women who love women. We call them LBW. For us the words mean "lesbian women", for everyone else it could mean "leg before wicket". When we are out walking or going somewhere, we observe the women around us and often try to guess if one of them might be lesbian. You can tell, you know, there is something about them, they look distinct.... We knew that your friend, the one who told you about us and brought you here, is one of us. She may be surprised that we could identify her like that, but we know, my daughters and I. We knew well what was going on between your friend and her friend. Very often the hiding we do is only in our heads.... People around us know. They are not stupid or blind. That is why I am saying, what does this term "best friend" that women use for one another really mean. Is it about sharing one's innermost feelings with someone, what does this friendship between women mean? All right, sometimes people cannot be sure that so-and-so woman is a lesbian, but you know what, in general people are uneasy about women who do not appear to be part of the usual scene.'

'There are many women in our families, single and married, who really love women. But it does not come out into the open. Religions, society, all condemn it. Who would like it to be exposed? Though there has been some change in recent times. A few days ago there was an article in the local newspaper, did you see it?' She looked at me, and as I shook my head she repeated, 'No? Chotu, do you remember it? On what date did it appear?'

Chotu had already opened the sideboard and was looking through a pile of old newspapers on the shelf. 'Chotu will find it for us. She keeps a lookout for all such stories,' Juhi said. Chotu quickly found the paper and passed it to me. It was in the local language. I passed the paper to Juhi who explained briefly what the article was about. It described a group that existed in a district not far from where we were. It also narrated how two women had got married to each other in another nearby semi-rural area. It advocated love between women as something positive.

'The first time I heard about woman-to-woman relationships was when a teacher who lived in our area left her husband within a few days of her marriage. She disappeared suddenly from the house one fine morning. All they found was a small note in her book in which she said she was leaving for good. There were all kinds of whispers about her being in love with another woman. Both of them had been forcibly married off. She had left her husband on account of her love for another woman. Looking back, I think it was a bold step. My girlfriend was forced to marry, I ended up marrying. None of us escaped marriage, or men, but this woman did. My friend and I, we were caught with one another by the family. To keep her from me, my friend's father even changed houses. Finally she was married off. She was so beautiful....'

Juhi sighed. 'Are you talking about Shashi?' Chotu asked.

'Yes. I have told my girls about her,' Juhi added, turning to me, then back to her daughter. 'Chotu, will you sit here and listen to us talk the whole day, or will you go and study?'

'I am going.'

Juhi continued, 'I was saying she was beautiful. She was fair, very fair. In contrast, she had thick black curly hair. When she spread that hair out it seemed like a dark net lay over her shoulders. The spread of her hair was so wide. She belonged to a high caste and came from a highly educated family. Her father was a professor and they belonged to the middle class. They were very comfortably off. She herself was so simple and lovable. We were nearly two years into our relationship when we were caught. We were in the middle of taking our Class XII examinations when her father saw the letters I had written to her. Of course we used to take the precaution of not signing our names on the letters. I used to sign as Jai. But even that got us into trouble. To protect herself, Shashi told her father that I had written the letters. She thought that since I was a girl, it would all be forgotten.'

'Shashi's father was educated. He was aware that love could exist between women. He simply took her away—the whole family moved to another locality. But I found my way there also. I would go there by bus. It took me about two hours to reach her locality.

I would stand in some fields from where I could see the house, and hide behind a tree after tying my kerchief to it, as a signal. She would make some excuse or the other to her family and come out. Thus we kept meeting under the tree. After some time when the family eased their control over her I began to go to her house. That year both of us failed the exams. Next year we took the exams again, and passed. We got admission in the same college but our subjects were different. We saw each other during the periods when we had to learn the compulsory subjects, like English and Sanskrit.'

'Then Shashi got engaged. I felt alone. I realised we would not be able to escape marriage. We had already been caught once, in our relationship. I began to seriously contemplate marriage. Shashi did not like the way I began to dress for college, I took to wearing *sarees*. She asked me why I was not wearing pants or a skirt. But by then I too had decided to marry and change my way of life.'

'But the strange thing was what my father made Shashi do. She got married before I did. When news of my marriage reached my father, he was so dead set against the match that he got Shashi and her family to file a charge of kidnapping against my husband...! Even today I wonder how they made her agree to be a part of their whole scheme. I saw them in the court. She would come with her husband. But there was no way I could ask her why she did what she did. Not that it really matters now.... Just one of those incomplete endings that leave one wistfully wondering why it happened, what happened to her and our friendship, knowing full well there will be no answering echo. We lost touch with each other long ago.'

'But my other friend Lucy—she was the first woman I loved. I tried to reconnect with her after my marriage fell through. I looked for her. But I could not meet her. No one seemed to know her whereabouts. I knew she had gone to South Africa. But I was not sure if she was still there.... Then a few months ago I learnt that she had passed away. It upset me. Then I suddenly ran into her sister at a funeral. I was meeting her after 22 years! We did not recognise each other. She had aged so much. She told me that I too looked older. I did not know how to ask about Lucy. So I asked her how her sisters were doing. Then she said that she and Lucy were fine but the youngest sister had passed away. I felt sorry. But I confess

I was so relieved that it was not Lucy. I mumbled a quick prayer for the other sister who had died. I could not ask her more about Lucy. But I made my own inquiries afterwards.'

'I had met Lucy at a family wedding. I was in Class X, about Chotu's age. You can imagine what an effect this had on me. When you are young there is such fire inside you, such passion. And this was my very first relationship. I can tell you relationships between women throw you off, they are so intense. My husband would often tell me that I was a cold woman. What did he know, men can never know what we feel. He did not believe that there could be relationships between women. He mocked the idea when once during the early days of our marriage I told him about my relationships with women. Later of course there was no point in sharing anything with him. But what a difference there is between man-woman and woman-woman relationships. There is no compulsion to have sex when you are with a woman. Sex itself is so different in the two relationships. Women understand one another and that understanding makes all the difference. A man's love is full of conditions. He is bred to make these demands in love. Women must produce children, and that too boys, and so on. The other advantage is that women can meet and love each other provided that no one suspects the real nature of the relationship. That is the danger. Secrecy is what makes these relationships possible, and also makes them a punishment. There are so few people you can talk with about this....'

'Though I felt attracted to women, it was from Lucy that I learnt about lesbianism. She lived in the hostel, and in hostels girls frequently have relationships with one another. We knew each other before our relationship developed. We had gone to attend the wedding of a common relative. When we met at this wedding we roamed around with our fingers entwined. When the wedding was over and only a handful of relatives were left, I fell asleep on the cot after dinner. Everyone was around. Lucy was sitting right next to me. She ran her fingers gently through my hair. It was a wonderful feeling. I opened my eyes and looked at her. She kissed me on my cheeks. Others around us did not pay much attention, it is quite common among us Christians to kiss each other on the cheek. She looked at me in that special way. She said, "Will you be my friend? I like you a lot."'

'I willingly agreed. I liked her a lot too. We had so much fun together. I never had a sister, and when I came to the city I missed my village. Having her for a friend was the best thing that happened to me. She would come to meet me regularly on a cycle. I did not know cycling. It was such a new thing for me to see a woman on a cycle. I loved to see her ride it. The picture that flashes before my eyes as I talk to you is of her slowing down on the bike. Her two tiny ponytails bobbing up and down, and then becoming still.... She is wearing a blue T-shirt and blue pants. I would wait for her each evening. We would sit and talk, flirting with one another, just sitting and holding hands. Then she would go back and I would be filled with sadness. Her style was just like Chotu's, if you know what I mean....'

'With all of this loving going on, I somehow cleared the Class X exams. She joined the College of Nursing. I would go there to meet her. She got involved with another woman there. When I went to meet Lucy her friend would get so angry, she would throw all her things down from the second floor. She was jealous of me. She would even hit Lucy, but Lucy would not retaliate. Finally, I withdrew. It did not make sense to me. Shashi showed interest in me, and we got involved with each other.'

'When I had just started seeing my husband, Lucy came to me one day. She told me she was leaving for South Africa and that if I wanted to come along, I could.... She left and I stayed on here. Sometimes I wonder how different life would have been had I taken that other road, of going with her....'

'You will understand now why I want my daughters to be able to choose freely. All of us deserve that chance, that one possibility of choosing from all the other possibilities put together.'

10

Hasina and Fatima

At the turbulent confluence of three northern rivers, Ganga, Yamuna and the mythological Saraswati that pushed its course underground a millennium ago, stands the ancient town of Allahabad, considered holy by Hindus. On the newly developed periphery of this old town, between the bungalows and flats of the rich, past the crossroads of village Beli to the right, is a forgotten space sloping over a wide *nallah*. On the slope a creaking door opens onto a courtyard. Right in the centre, towards the back, stands a rectangular building constructed in the colonial style, with a verandah running alongside supported by pillars. From it stare five unblinking rooms.

In two of the rooms live Hasina Bano, her friend Fatima and Fatima's friend Choti. Untangled from amongst these lives, this is the story of Hasina Bano and her relationship with Fatima.

The norms and pressures of marriage, traditional family structures and daily struggles of material survival intersect with moments of inexplicable transcendence, built around the love between these two women. Their difficult times, their giving and taking, their mutual support, their interdependence, cannot all be classified as one identity, or contained in one. Therefore, our effort in presenting the facts as they are is problematic. We see the intimate connection between these two women as an example of how fluid the lines are between a sexual relation and an emotional bond. We read a lesbian identity, impose an orientation, rely on a conditioned perception. We admit that our purpose of rendering this particular 'lesbian' identity visible comes up against peculiar complications. Such a deep-rooted, flexible and sustained interweaving of consciousnesses and destinies, evidenced in this story, defies the simple narration of supposedly simple facts.

Our own ideological need to establish a single identity for our subjects in this context is countered by our interaction with such women, whose lives are proof that no one identity fully expresses even limited truths. Facing these inevitable contradictions, we have tried to narrate the story of Hasina Bano, a story that refutes easy interpretation and convenient categorisation.

When we first walked down the narrow lane into the courtyard and from there stepped into Hasina's room, neither she nor Fatima nor Choti was there. But there was a spirit of happiness hovering around the place that day, and it persisted through our visit.

Tahira, Hasina's youngest daughter, warmly welcomed us. Serving us tea and a snack of *murmure*, she introduced the people who shared that space. 'The government has banned the use of plastic bags, that is why we are all sitting here now, making these packets of paper. We'll earn something sitting at home. At least something is better than nothing.... That little thatched hut you see there, right in the corner of the compound, that is where Fatima keeps the load of bananas for ripening in a certain powder before selling them. She made the hut in the corner because the powder in which the bananas ripen has an overpowering stench. From here she carries them to the *kachehri* compound for sale.'

'Who helps her? Does she carry them by herself?' we asked.

'No, her relative from her village and her friend Choti also live here, together they take them,' Tahira said. She put her arm around the young girl sitting next to her, about twelve years old. 'Adjoining Fatima's room lives Hiralal mistri. This is his daughter. When she was very young her mother passed away, and now there are just the two of them, father and daughter... In the room near theirs lives the tempo *wala chacha* with his wife Vimla and three children.... That room there, the only one with a door, that locked iron blue door, the first one from the other side, it belongs to our landlady. She is the third wife of her husband. This space, land, house, everything, her husband has given her. Inside where she lives there is a bathroom, kitchen, everything. She is more fortunate than we are, we all have to sleep in one room, only Ammi and Fatima sleep outside. The landlady worked in a school as a teacher. She lives alone now. Though for some time now she has not been living here, she has gone to her daughter....'

'Last year when there were floods and our house was inundated we climbed up and sat on the roof, you see these walls of bricks,' Tahira added, pointing to the unfinished door frames, windows and walls above us. 'After the floods the old landlady came and started to get these built, but without completing the work she left. At that time we pleaded with her to get our part repaired first. This house is old and falling apart, it is not in such a condition that anyone can just add another floor to it. Anytime it can collapse. What will happen to us then? We alone will have to bear the brunt. If there is a flood again we won't be able to sit on the roof even. This year it didn't rain much, otherwise what would have happened! Fatima and Hiralal mistriji worked on this construction themselves.' Tahira's voice had a ring of complaint, as if these two had somehow let the occupants down.

Along with the many humans in the congested compound live Fatima's faithful dog Moti and Hasina's pets: hens, rabbits, chicks, a parrot, and a charming little frisky baby goat. Before we left, we asked Tahira to tell her mother we had come and would return to see her.

The next time we went Hasina was home. She wore a saree. Her head was uncovered. Her long earrings chimed to her movements as she greeted us with a '*Salaam!*' She rose and pushed aside the heap of clothes piled on the string cot, inviting us to sit. She was just a little over four feet tall, and seemed much younger than her 40 years. Perhaps she gave that impression because of her smile— it spread in the happiest way I have ever seen, mocking the lines of tension around her mouth, while crinkles at the corners of her eyes deepened mischievously, almost dangerously. In contrast to her daughters who spoke standard Hindustani, she spoke mainly in the local dialect mixed with Urdu, sweet to the ear, lyrical and intimate.

Lifting her smiling brown eyes, Hasina shared the moment of her first meeting with Fatima, in a whisper. 'I was standing by the well in the *kachehri* compound one day, all dressed up in red. At that time he emerged from the well and told me, "I love you". He came for me disguised as a woman and cast on me a magical spell I cannot explain. I cannot live without her. She has not come from your and my world, she has come from the world of the spirits.'

When she spoke of Fatima, Hasina sometimes referred to her as a man and sometimes as a woman. A bit stunned as well as moved by her description, we were silent for a few seconds and she remained lost in her reverie. Then she continued in a normal tone: 'I was born in a village called Chitaymau and grew up with two sisters and one brother. Our father was poor. He had ten *bighas* of land. In my childhood I got a chance to go to school. I can read Urdu. My sister lived in purdah but I would go around without wearing any *burqa*, nor did I cover my face. I used to take the goats out for grazing. My sister would grumble that I did nothing in the kitchen except want food all the time. At that time I could not hold back my hunger. And today...' she paused thoughtfully, '...today it has all changed. The man my sister is married to, his family wanted me as the bride. I was fairer than my sister and they wanted a fair-complexioned girl. But my family decided I would not be good for that house because there was no woman there, and since I did not show interest in household chores, they thought I would not be able to manage the domestic work. But look at me today, I not only do the domestic work, I also go out to work. I am running my own life. I am proud of myself.'

'Days passed, years went by, now only our mother is alive. She lives with my sister in the village. My brother is in Bangalore in a casting factory for brass. And I'm here, with each passing year growing older. I am no longer as fair and agile, you know how with age everything changes. My whole body aches. Each day I have to take a pill that costs two rupees, so that the pain eases. I have this nervous feeling inside me, there are times when I just feel like running away. Previously I was always cheerful. Even now I don't like to go around with a long face. But at times I can't help it....'

'I came to the city for my livelihood. I took up massaging as my job. But I cannot count on it, there may be work, there may not be work, nothing about it is certain. Now I have taken work in two houses where I work for Rs 300 a month in each house, sweeping and swabbing floors and cleaning utensils. Both mistresses stood by me in my recent hour of need. Just now I went back to work after a month but they did not hire anyone else in my place. They said, "We'll have only you to work for us." They like me because it is not my habit to gossip or carry tales from one house to the other.

The master of one of the houses works in the Middle East. When he is here he says, "Don't use so many utensils, Khala will have trouble washing so many." They respect me in that house. It's there that I have my first cup of tea in the morning, and *nashta*. They don't let me leave without eating something. They even come to my house to inquire about our welfare….'

'You can't imagine this house when Fatima and I moved into it, it was very filthy then. This compound was used as if it was no more than a toilet. All the neighbours from around came here to ease themselves, morning and evening. We cleaned it with our own hands. Then only did this place become fit for human occupation. Our second daughter Sahira—you know Sahira, the one who works with me in your friend's house, the friend who told you about us— Sahira does not understand, she does not want to understand. She keeps saying, "Look for another room somewhere else." Tell me, how can we take another room, just like that, simply take another room, how can we? It is not that simple, take another room, indeed. Admitted that a door is missing and the rain drips from the ceiling. I've put a curtain in the verandah, it blocks the cold in the winter and in summer the breeze blows in freely so it is cool. For the rainy season I've tied a plastic sheet under the ceiling, that takes care of the dripping water. A room anywhere else costs nothing less than Rs 500–600 per month. We're paying practically nothing here. Whatever we save I put away for Sahira's wedding. The woman who is to be her mother-in-law wants her married on Id, after the *roza*s. I want it postponed a bit, When our little goat Chandni gets all her teeth she will fetch Rs 1,000–1,500. We will sell her on Bakr-Id, for the sacrifice. God willing, we can earn a little bit.'

We said, 'We have heard that the boy Sahira is engaged to does not work. Is it necessary to marry her off to him?' Hasina explained, 'The work one does comes and goes, but it is the duty of all parents to get their children married off. The command of the Lord is that women marry and beget children. On the Day of Judgement I will have to give an account of all the things that I had to do and did not do. Our Sahira, she can read and write. She regularly recites the *namaaz* and observes the *roza*s.' She said it in a flat tone, as if she was not impressed with all that reading. I looked at her to ascertain from her face what her tone indicated but Hasina had moved on.

'Ayesha, my daughter older to Sahira, was married off to my sister's *devar*. A daughter was born, and a few days after that Ayesha passed away. The daughter is gone but one feels like giving things to the granddaughter, she is the only memory of my daughter. I've bought things for her. These things alone cost Rs 300–400. I've only one son, Firoz. He always manages to find some job or the other but he doesn't regularly work. Someone has cast a spell on him. So I sent him to the *maulvi*. He has given him a talisman. Thank God he is working now. He is employed in a biscuit-cake factory at Rajapur. His pay is not in proportion to the labour he is asked to put in. But I think the regularity of work will make him disciplined. Attending to a job daily will slowly put an end to his vagabond habits and also keep him away from the bad company he's fallen into.'

'You see, now I'm the only one around to look after all my children. Alone, I have to take on all the work that has to be done. That is why I say I cannot leave Fatima. She is really brave, what man can match her courage? When we were on the roof during the floods, a snake crawled up to exactly where we were sitting. All of us were so shocked, we couldn't move. It was Fatima and Fatima alone who could have done what she did. With the presence of mind she has, she caught hold of the snake with her bare hands and killed it. No man, old or young, can stand up to her. One night some youths were being chased by the police and they jumped over the wall into the compound. They were wandering about the streets and the patrol got after them. But Fatima settled it well and proper, while we all slept.'

We expressed our wish to meet a strong woman like Fatima, and asked Hasina if she would mind our writing about her. Hasina raised a restraining hand, quickly explaining, 'Fatima is not the kind of person who will talk to anyone. She stands no nonsense. She is a stern woman. If a fellow even slightly suggests anything improper to a woman, or tries to swear or whistle or sing a line or make a pass, she puts him in his place there and then. One cannot take liberties with Fatima. At times when I work longer than usual or am held up somewhere and do not return home on time, she comes looking for me from house to house. She would not approve of the way I am sitting and talking to you now.'

We wanted to see Fatima, so the next day we went to the *kachehri* compound, the site of the well where Hasina had first met her. The *kachehri* was entirely a man's world. The well was hidden from view by the crowds surrounding it, concealed in the same manner that the well-water was hidden by the structure's walls and canopy. Only on pushing our way close to it were we able to see the circular empty space between the bodies of dozens of men. 'The water dried up many years ago,' someone told us, 'but no one has boarded up the well.' The advocates in their white ties and black coats, holding pens and paper and thick dusty files, though busy with their clients, could not keep their eyes off us. We were a distracting and unaccustomed presence in this place of men where Hasina and Fatima, two women, had instantaneously accepted their love for each other.

How had it come about, the chance of their finding one another among this busy, alien throng, how had they recognised the nature of their profound connection? Given the context, almost impossible! Yet we accept this as the true account of their meeting. Our observation of the actual well and Hasina's description of it, her transformative encounter with Fatima, the radical moment of the other's emergence from unseen and unknown depths underground, 'the world of the spirits', did not coincide. Interweaving her facts with the logic of fantasy, sublimity, dream and magic, Hasina had gone beyond the limits of the socially permissible. Paradoxically, in a male-dominated location where male-inspired and male-authored laws were interpreted and applied by men in favour of men, her vision was rooted in the realm of the illegal. Somehow, either miraculously or through sheer strength of will, she had generated possibility from the matrix of the impossible. Her private world materialised its substance from the very same public ground that completely excluded both her and her desired other.

Barely a few yards from the wrangling disorder of the *kachehri*, vendors and peddlers stood along the road. Among them, as far as the eye could see, Fatima and her friend Choti were the only two women among men hawking their goods. Short and stout, wearing a cotton saree, Choti stood talking to Fatima. Somewhat dark and lean, in a *salwar-kameez*, *dupatta* tied around her head, with one raised foot set on a sack and the other on the ground, Fatima stood sorting bunches of bananas. The large man's watch strapped on her wrist caught the August sun in the middle of its round dial and shone back little signals of light.

We went up to Fatima and asked her the price of the bananas. Pointing to different heaps she stated the various prices for the various kinds. We asked her to reduce the price. But she refused. Ignoring us, she went back to the task of pulling out, arranging and rearranging the different piles. We bought the bananas at the price she demanded, and left. The next day we told Hasina we had met Fatima. She smiled and asked, 'Did she ask you anything or say anything at all?'

'No,' we replied.

Hasina said, 'I told you, she will not talk. Where does she have the time? Her work is so hard. Carrying that load morning and evening, there is a pain in her ribs. She does not keep well. In the morning the man with a *thela* drops off the bananas, shouting "a thousand bananas". And he pockets the money for a thousand bananas. But the number always turns out to be less. No one can do anything about this thievery. How much can you fight? They will give the bananas to someone else if you argue. Her income depends entirely on what she can sell. When she can't sell them all in the *kachehri* she stands at the Beli crossroads. It is best when the entire lot of bananas get sold by the evening. If they are not sold and have to be kept overnight, we run into a loss because they become dark and pulpy. The next day they have to be sold at a much lower price. Fatima's son and her friend Choti both help her. But they don't wait till the evening at the Beli crossroads. They return home and Fatima comes later when she has sold them all....'

'But', we interrupted, 'Tahira was saying that the person who stays with Fatima is her relative from the village, not her son. If Fatima did not marry, who is that...?' We left the sentence unfinished. Horrified, Hasina tugged at her earlobes with thumb and forefinger, exclaiming, '*Tauba, tauba*! What are you saying? Fatima was married. Her husband died. That is the truth. My Tahira, she does not know. Fatima was married and this boy you think is her relative is her son.'

Observing Hasina's shock and her instinctive response to our query, we realised how sensitive this ground was. Such marginalised women struggling for daily survival had broken the traditional paradigm of the one-man/one-woman family, yet in no circum-stances could they freely articulate their choices. Hasina was well aware of the extent a woman of her class, whether Muslim, Hindu, Christian or Dalit, would be permitted to live in the way she wanted to. She was also aware that to violate the social norms was, in literal and psychological terms, a dangerous action that could have serious consequences. Hence there was also a strong need to claim the protection of the traditional paradigm. Maybe that is why she repeatedly referred to marriage as the right thing to do. She was simultaneously making Fatima out to be different from the norm by claiming that she came from the world of the spirits, and erasing that difference by asserting that she had once been married, and thus was assimilated into the norm. It was clear that Hasina felt pressured to seek legitimacy for her friend and for herself.

Whatever the facts, it was also very clear that the two women depended on each other. Hasina said, 'Her support is crucial in my life. I count on her. One day some years ago, as usual I went to work. Tahira was busy in the house. I left at seven in the morning as I always do after having my quota of *paan*. Fatima told me later how Firoz and Tahira had quarreled. Tahira told Firoz to carry the lid of the container when he went to get milk, so the milk would not spill over. Firoz ignored her. He does not like to get up early in the morning and do errands, and on top of that, take orders from a girl. Reluctantly he stepped down from the verandah to go for milk, and as he pushed his foot into his slippers Tahira rushed out calling after him, but he was not listening. She called out to him again, then she ran after him carrying the lid in her hand. When she was about a foot from him she reached out to grab his arm, and he lost his temper. He turned and jerked her hand so hard that the lid fell. Brother and sister took hold of each other like wrestlers, circling like the lid spinning on the ground. When one lifted a hand the other seized it and swore retaliation. Who was there to intervene? Fatima heard them shouting and came out from her room. Just then accidentally Firoz's foot fell on a sharp piece of broken glass. He began to bleed, and bleed profusely. Fatima took hold of him and sat him down, winding a cloth tightly around his foot. Then she took him to the hospital, got the dressing done, got medicine, got him a tetanus shot. On the way to the hospital she told one of our acquaintances to let me know there was a serious fight in the house, that I was not to worry but I must come home as soon as possible. When I reached home after receiving the message, I got nervous seeing so much blood splashed all over. After they returned home from the hospital I started scolding the children, but Fatima told me not to shout otherwise the situation would flare up again. I kept quiet.'

'Do you see? After all, why should she be concerned in my affairs! Yet she intervened in the fight, bandaged my son, took him to the hospital, got him treated. What would have happened had she not stepped in? She cares for me. There seems to be some previous connection between us, I cannot explain it. Sometimes when I've gone to my village or when she goes away and I don't see her, it seems as though I've lost something that is integrally mine. One day early in the morning I left for work. On the way I met someone coming from my village. He informed me my father was not well. I immediately set out for my village. Fatima returned home from selling bananas in the evening. She did not find me in the house. She had some food prepared by the landlady and fed Firoz. Next morning at six o'clock she left for my village. She came to find out how I was. She cares for my feelings. I join her family in times of happiness and sorrow.'

'We have lived together for nearly eight years and not once have we fought. With my husband there used to be a fight every day. She came to live next to us, in the place I lived in earlier. Then she was selling vegetables. She saw my husband, the trouble he created for me, the daily thrashings and bickerings. That set off our friendship. My husband has left me and gone. Now I have no support except for her. She does not leave me, nor do I leave her. She has a heart of gold. If she were rich she would help with money as well. Anyone may ask me to leave her, but I will not leave her ever. Why should I not live with someone who supports me in all ways?'

We asked, 'Why is this coming up again and again, the question of your leaving Fatima? Has anyone said anything to you?'

Hasina would not meet our eyes. She busied herself pushing her bangles up and down her arm. Finally she remarked with reluctance, 'I'm just saying it, that's all. My husband left me and went away. People have ideas of social status and family honour, they are critical of me, saying that I go out of the house and work for other people to earn my living. But if I don't work, should I eat the mud off the walls? My husband has gone, I need to eat, don't I? I have to work and I work honestly and with self-respect. What wrong am I doing? I tell you, my flesh and bones may turn to dust but I won't marry again.'

Observing her defensiveness and discomfort, we began to understand what she was struggling to conceal, the grudge her family held against her for her unwavering commitment to Fatima. We learnt of the actual tension in more detail when Hasina and Sahira began to keep different work times at the house of our friend, a local resident who had functioned as our intermediary. Our friend asked Hasina for more time and help. But Hasina worked elsewhere also. So our friend asked Sahira to help. Now that the daughter's work took more time, she began staying after the mother left. Alone with our friend, she was able to build a bond of greater trust and confidentiality.

One day she finally gave vent to her feelings. 'I am fed up with Ammi! I wonder what spell Fatima has cast on her, Ammi has turned insane. Thank God I read my *namaaz* and pray, if Fatima tries to work some black magic on me, I will be protected. What nonsense Ammi goes around talking! After she met this woman, this Fatima, she turned Abba out of the house. I don't even talk to her now. How many times I've told Ammi to take a house somewhere else! Live away from Fatima, get away from her! But she won't listen. She won't leave her. She will not listen to any of us, her own daughters, she listens to Fatima only. No matter what her children tell her, she will not listen. I don't like all this…!'

And then gradually, as Sahira began to work for our friend for longer periods, it became harder and harder to talk to Hasina about Fatima, or ask her anything about herself or their relationship. When the subject came up, she evaded it. Gradually she withdrew. Then one day after completing her work she pulled her veil over her face and left. She did not return.

'Ammi is running a fever,' was all Sahira would say.

www.ingramcontent.com/pod-product-compliance
Lightning Source LLC
Chambersburg PA
CBHW032351280326
41935CB00008B/525